PICTURE BOOK OF
PUPPIES

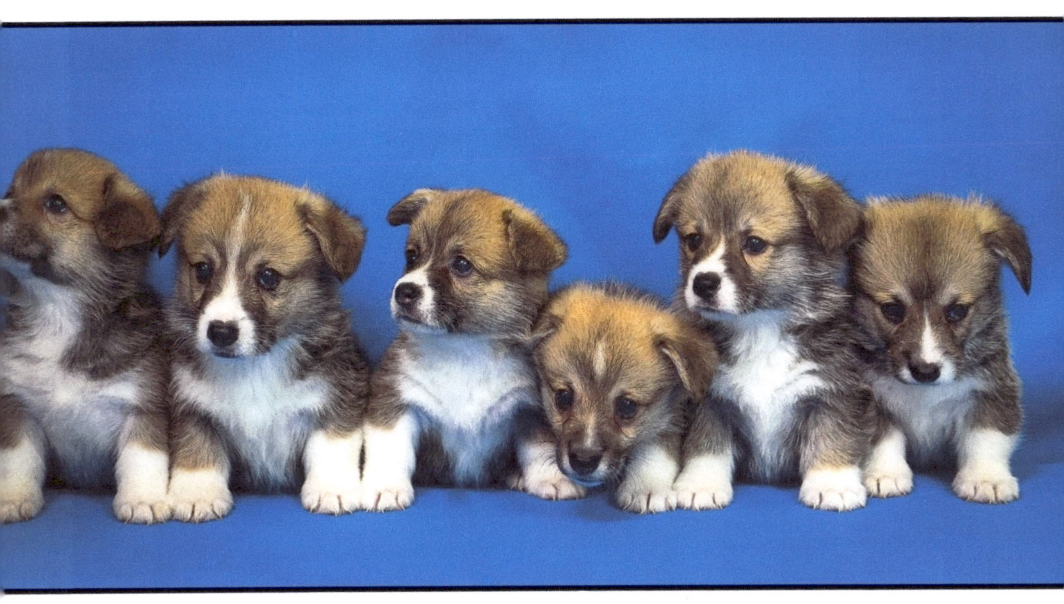

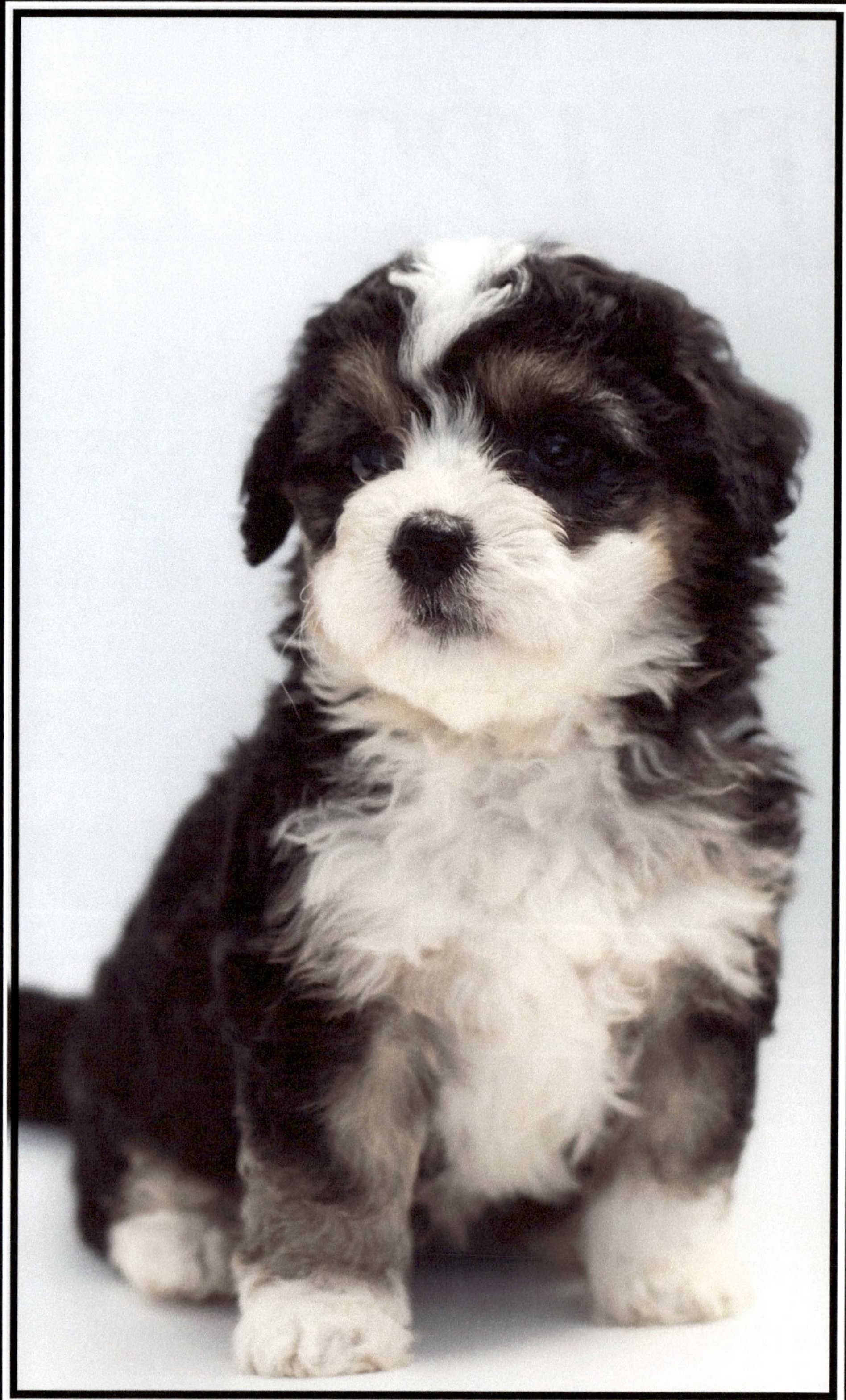

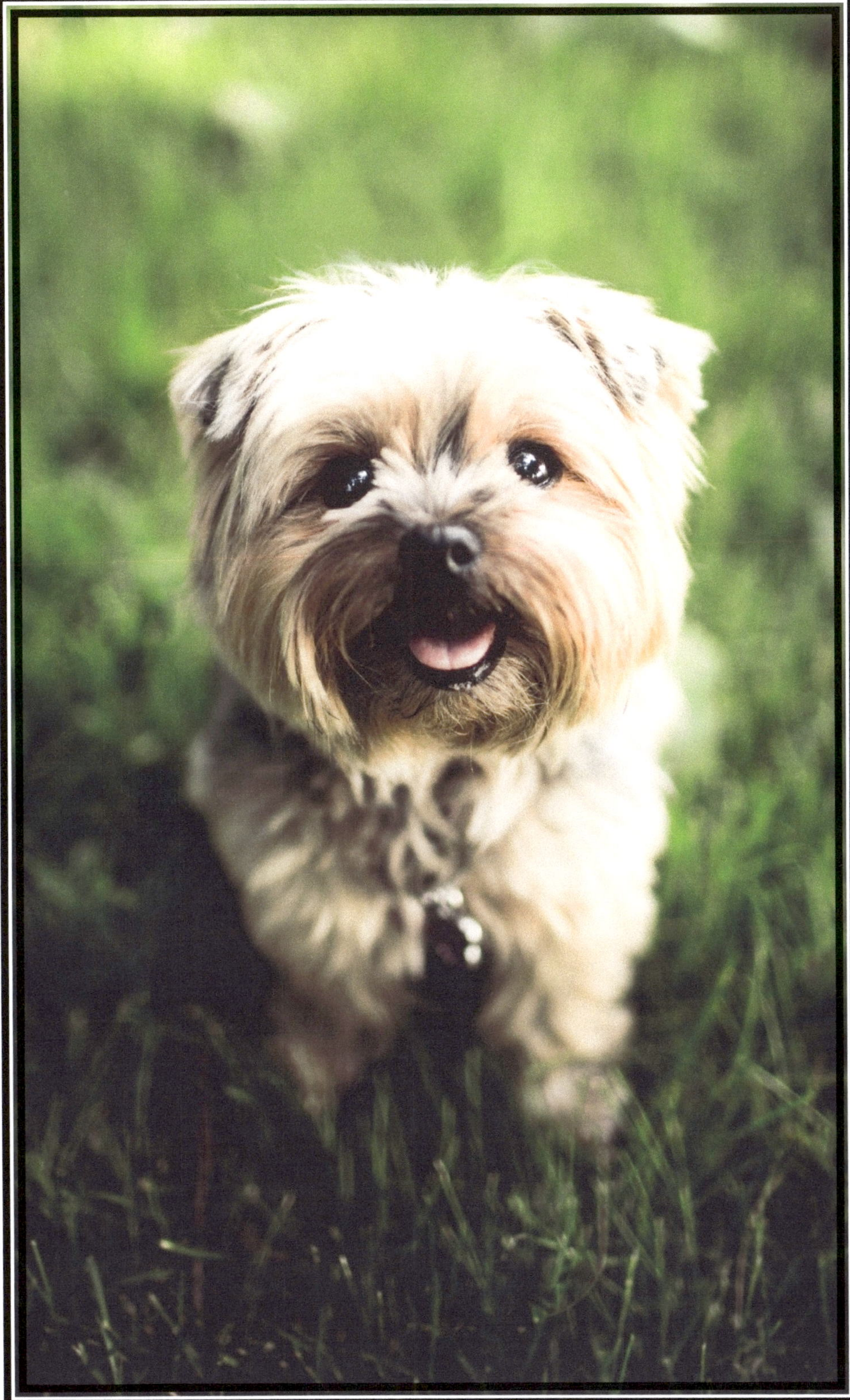

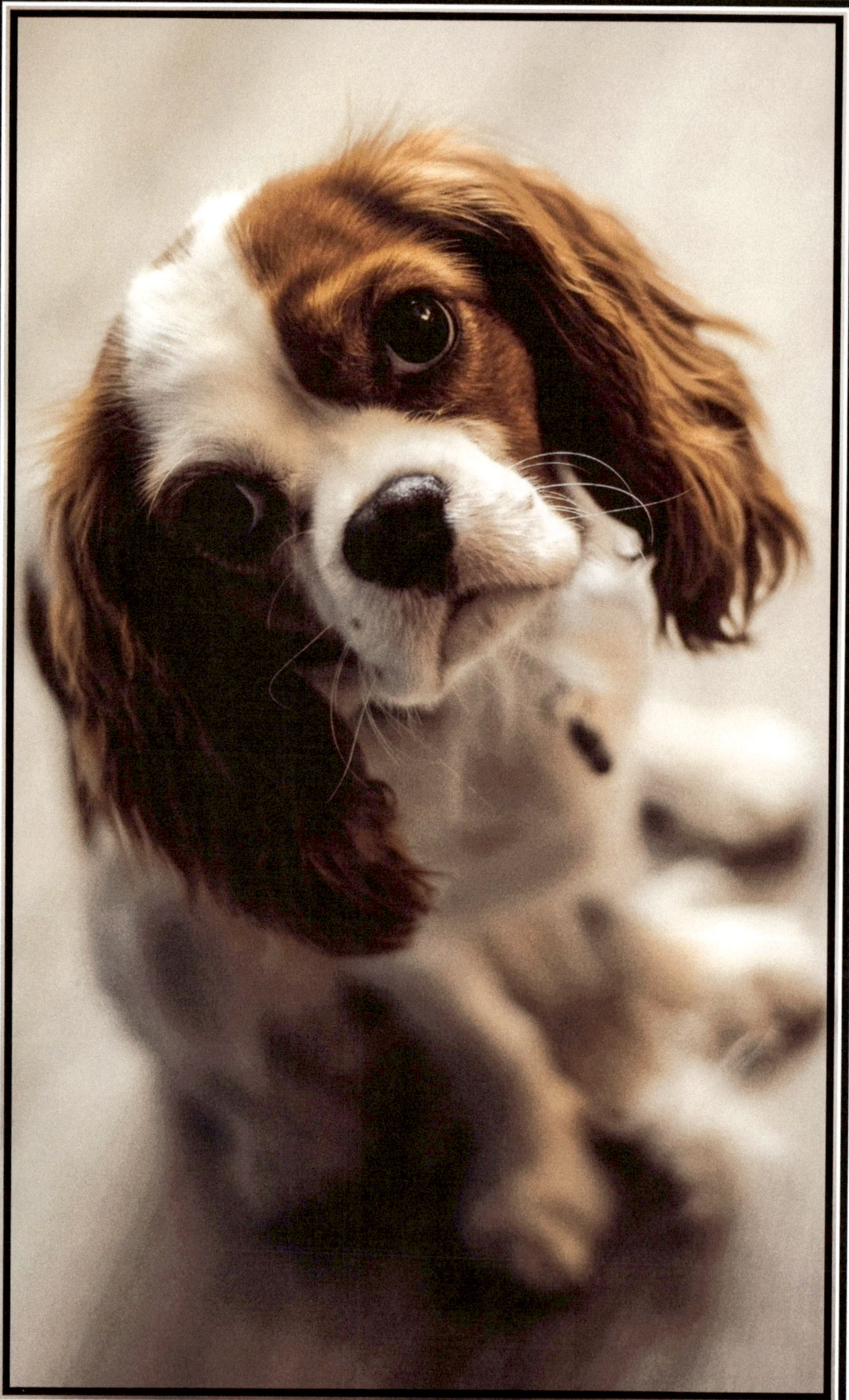

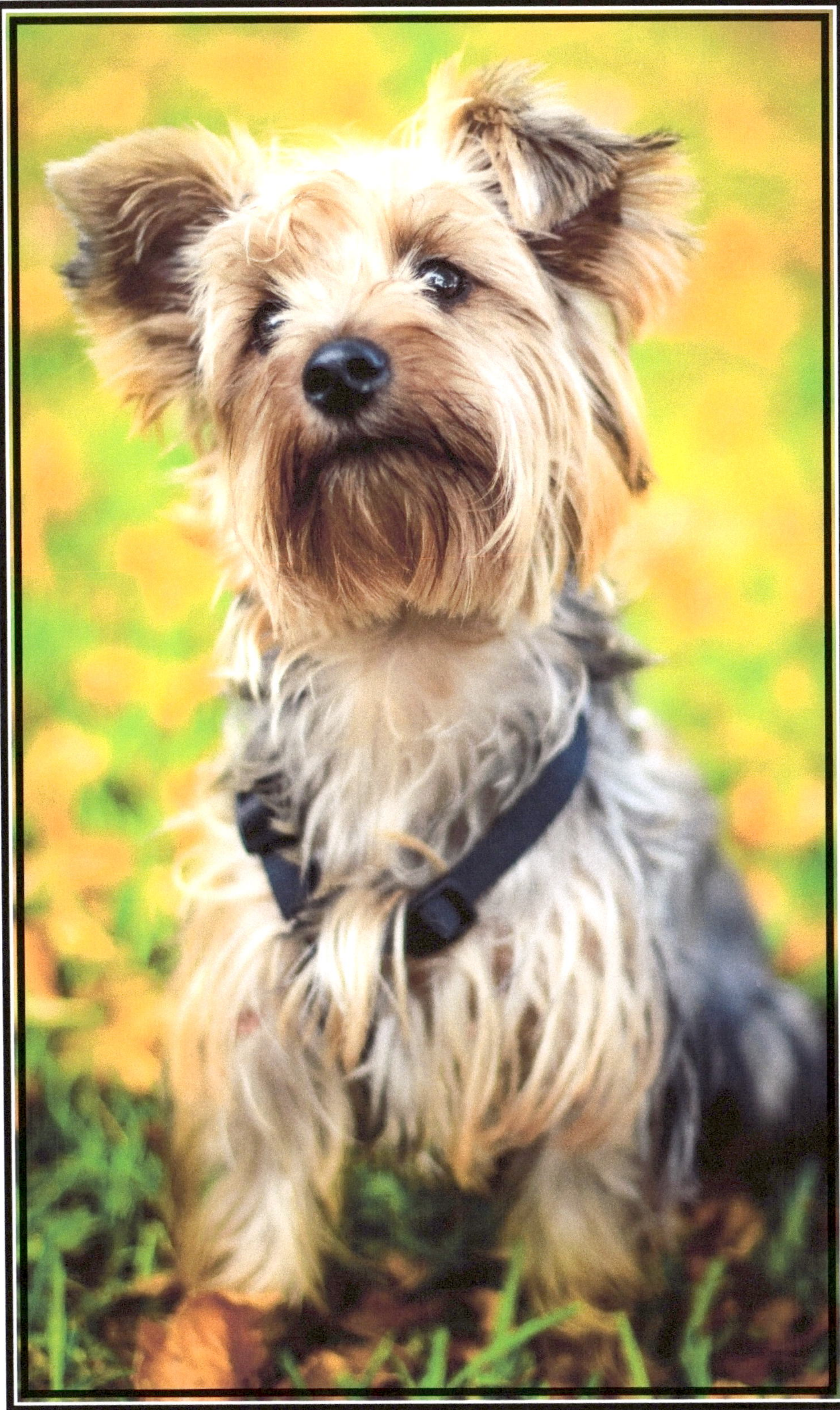

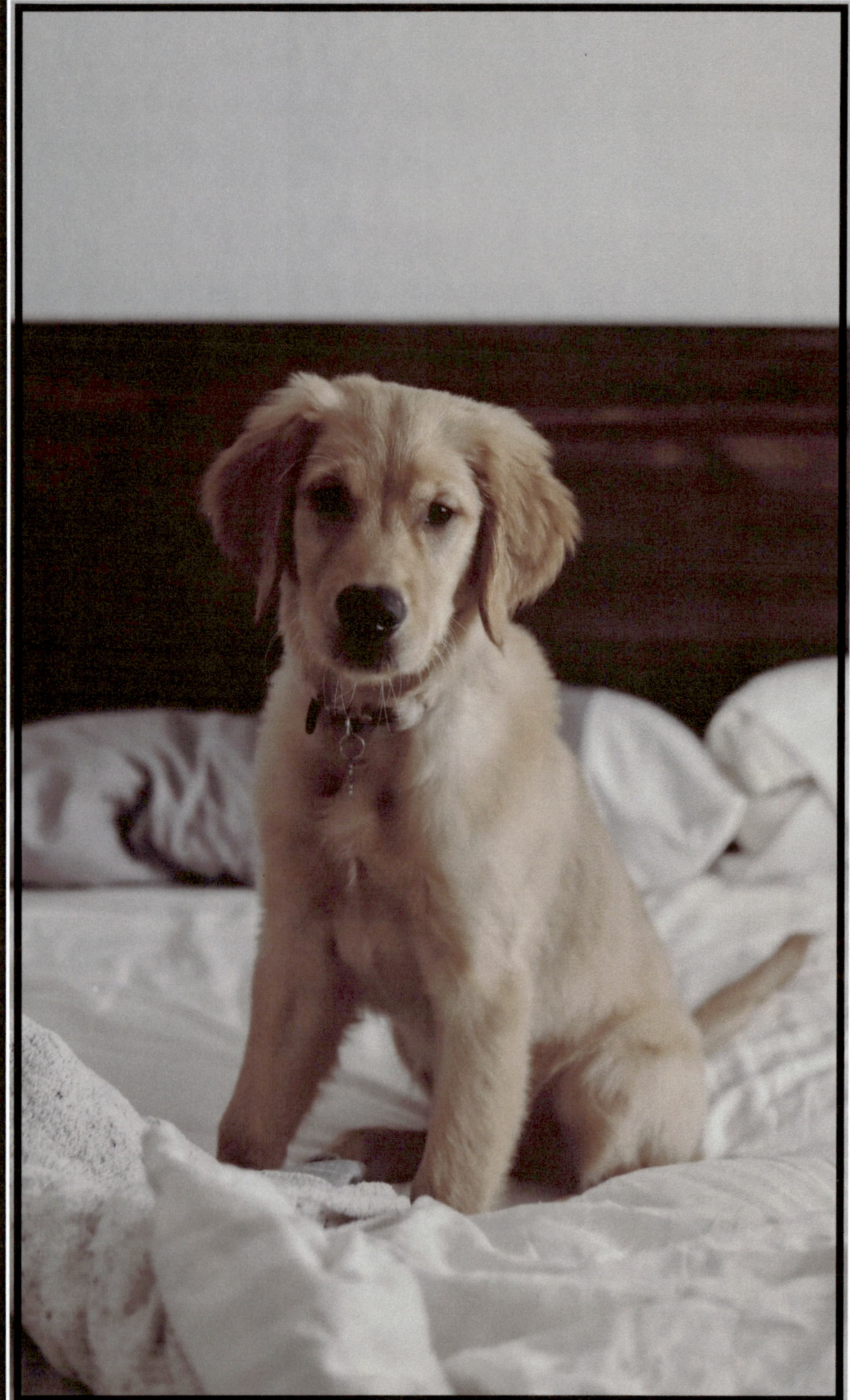

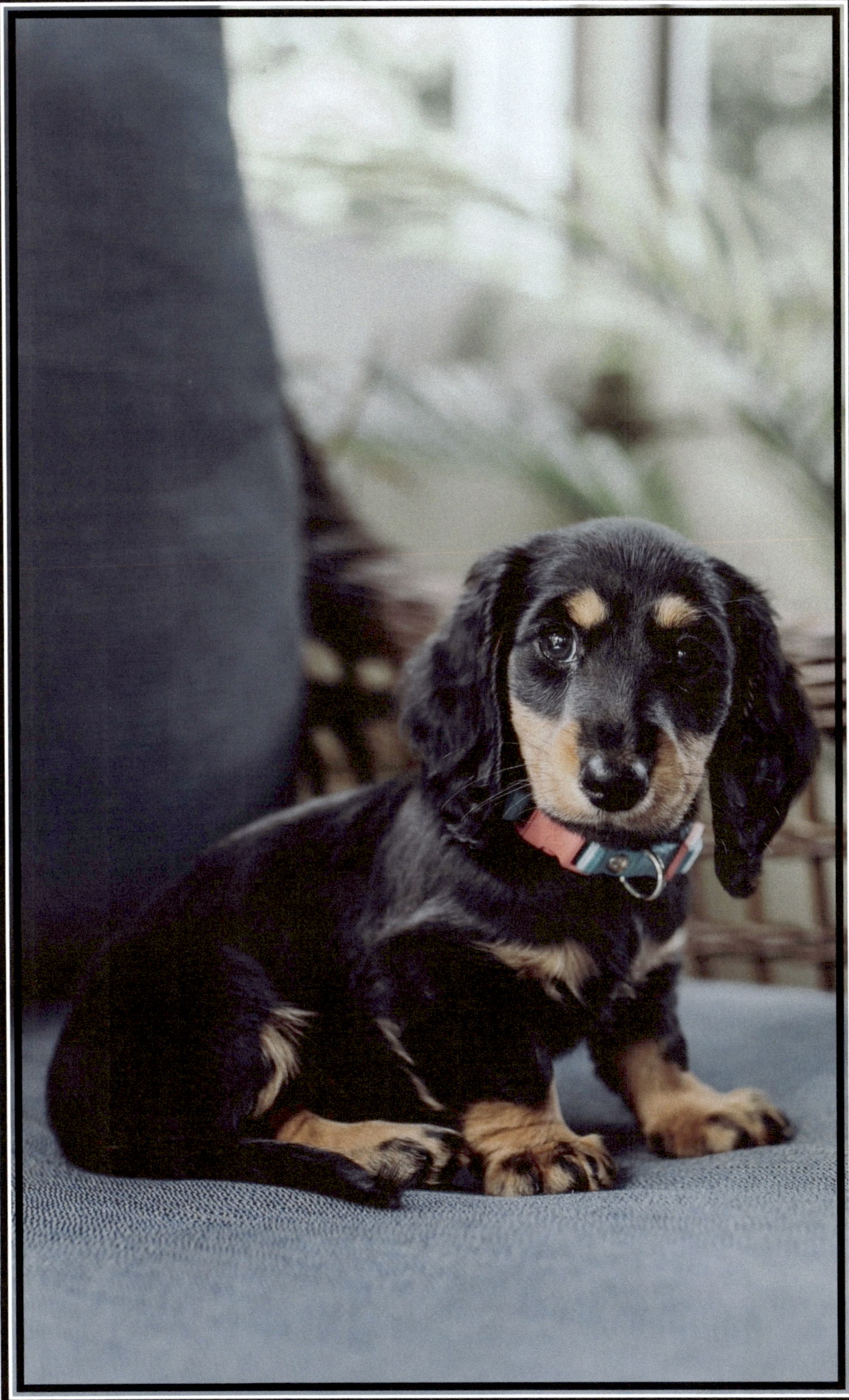

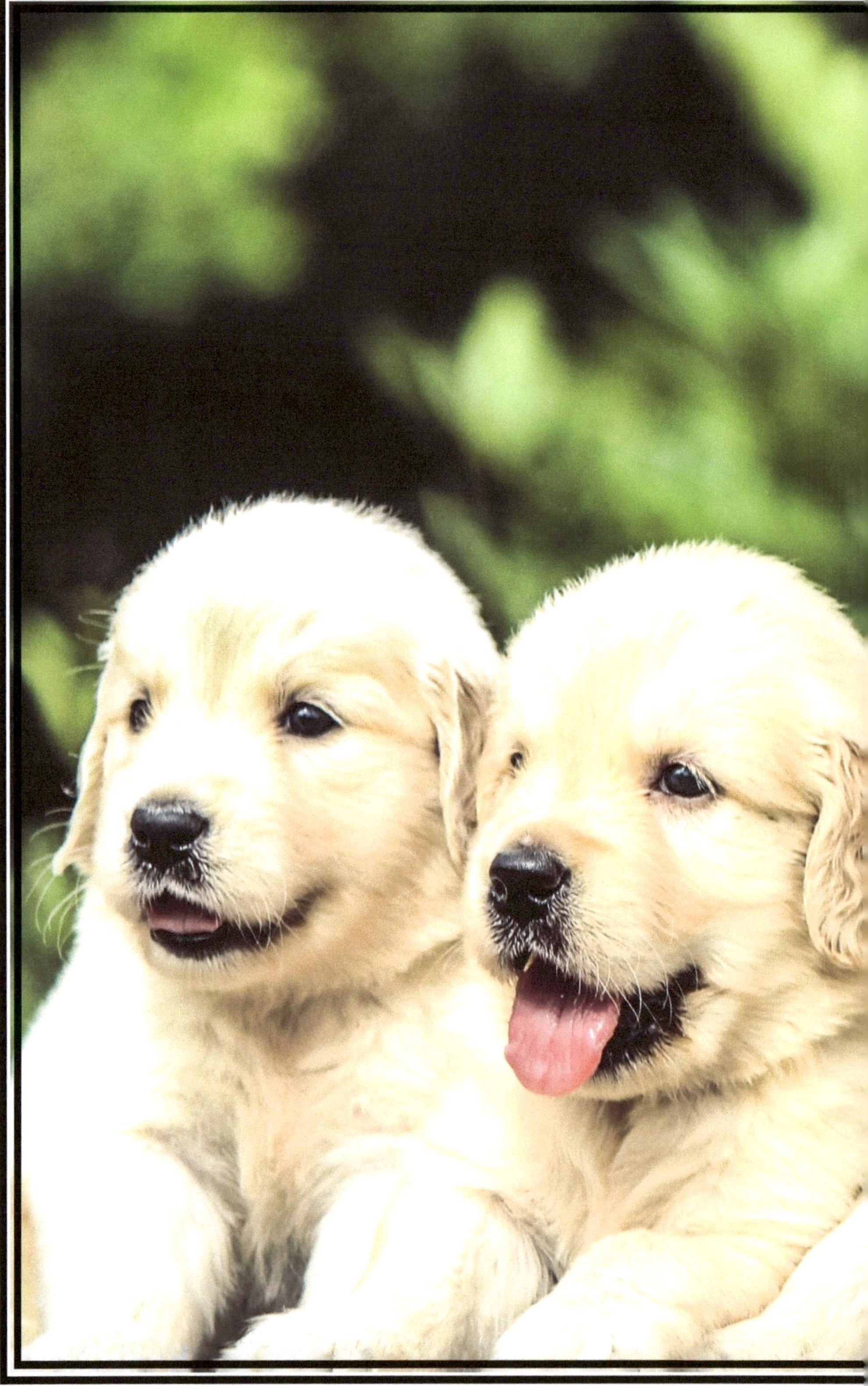

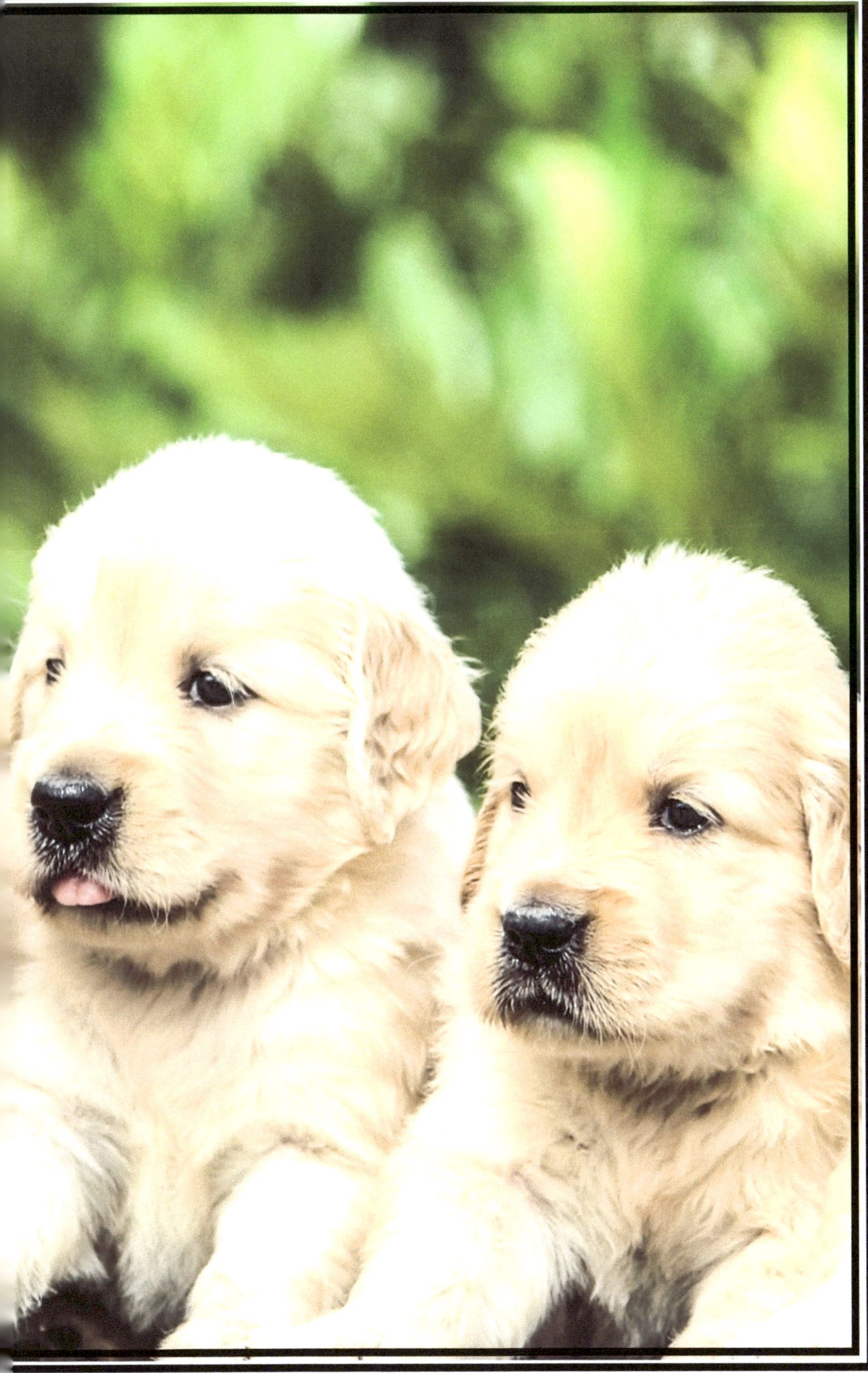

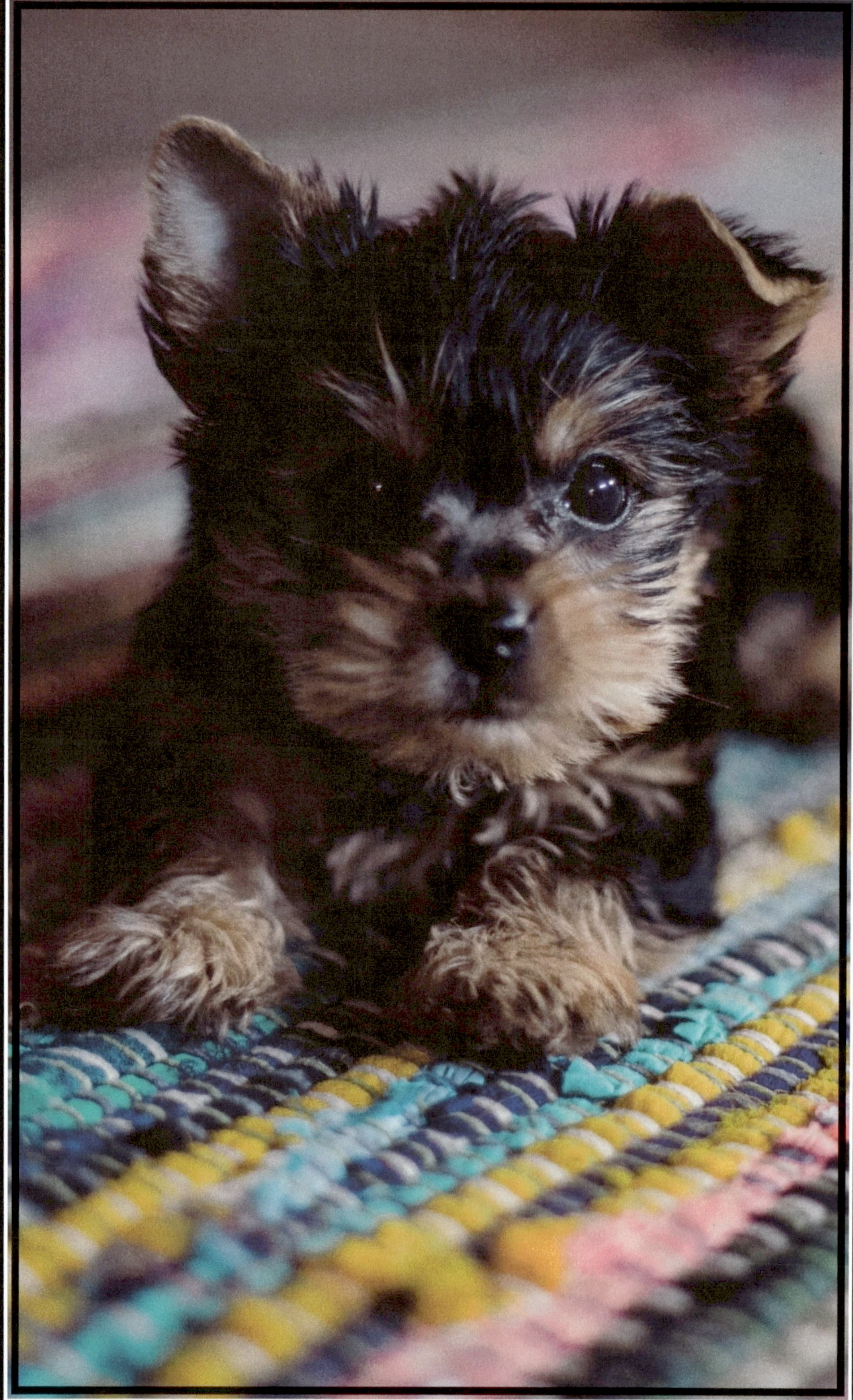

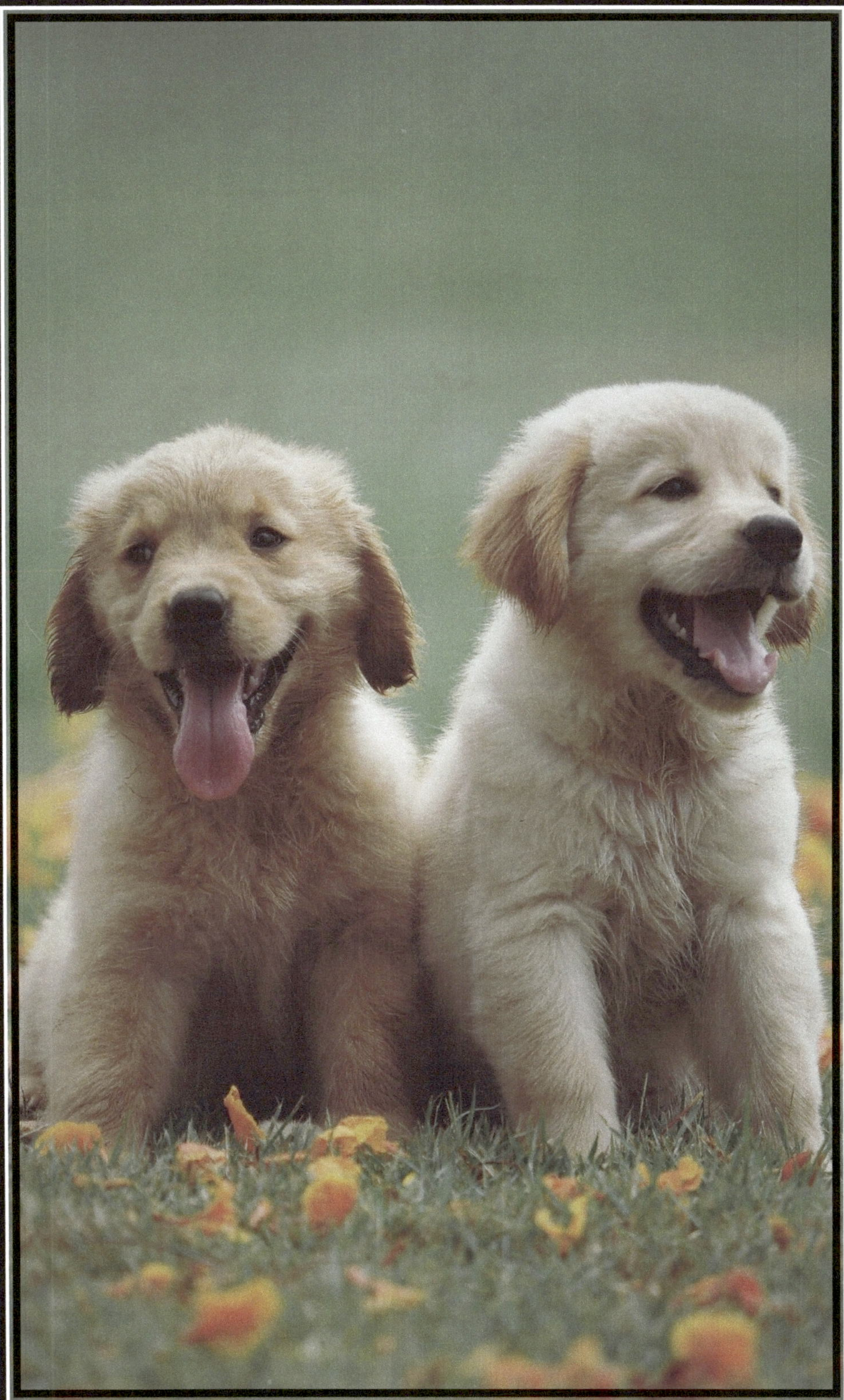

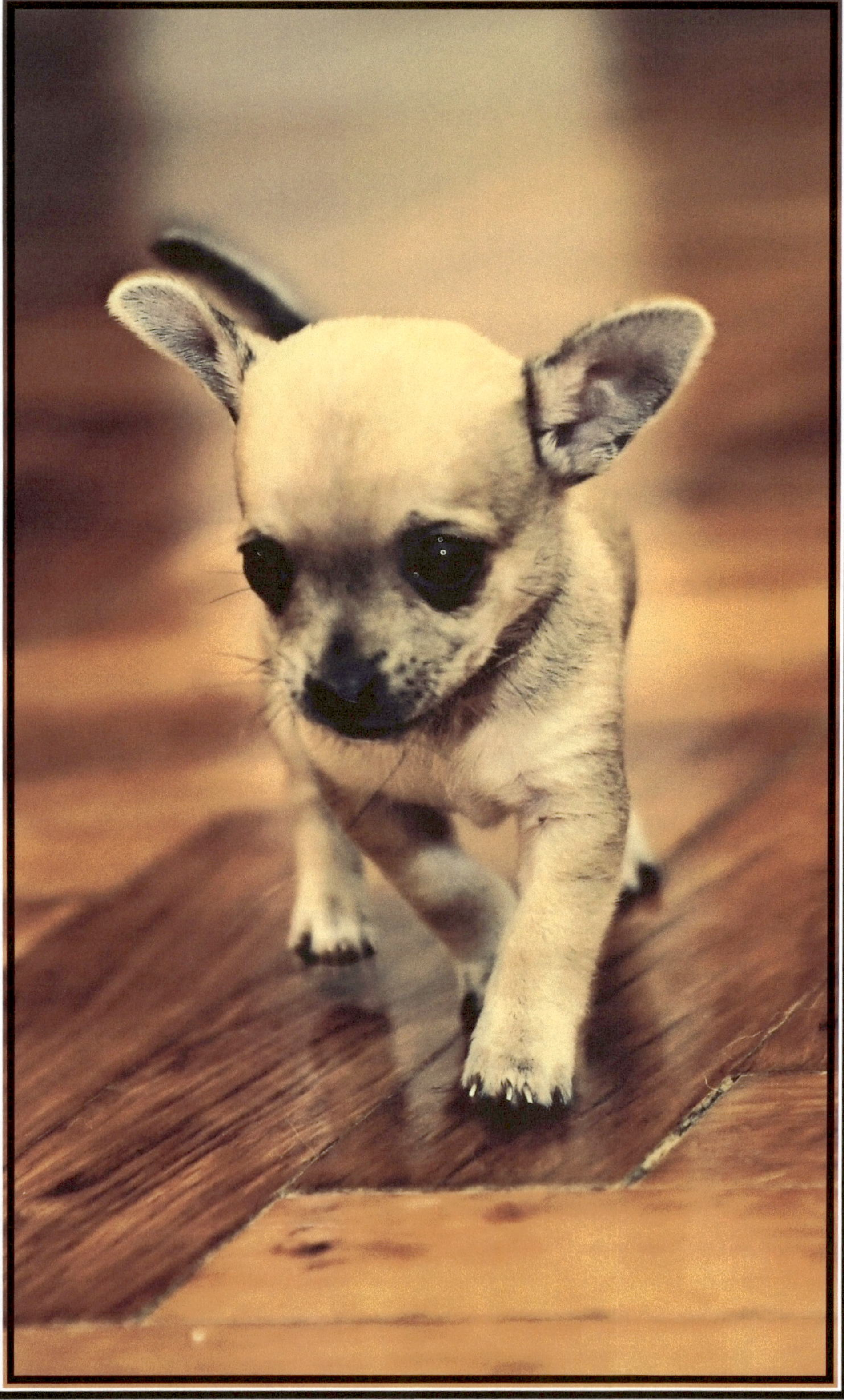

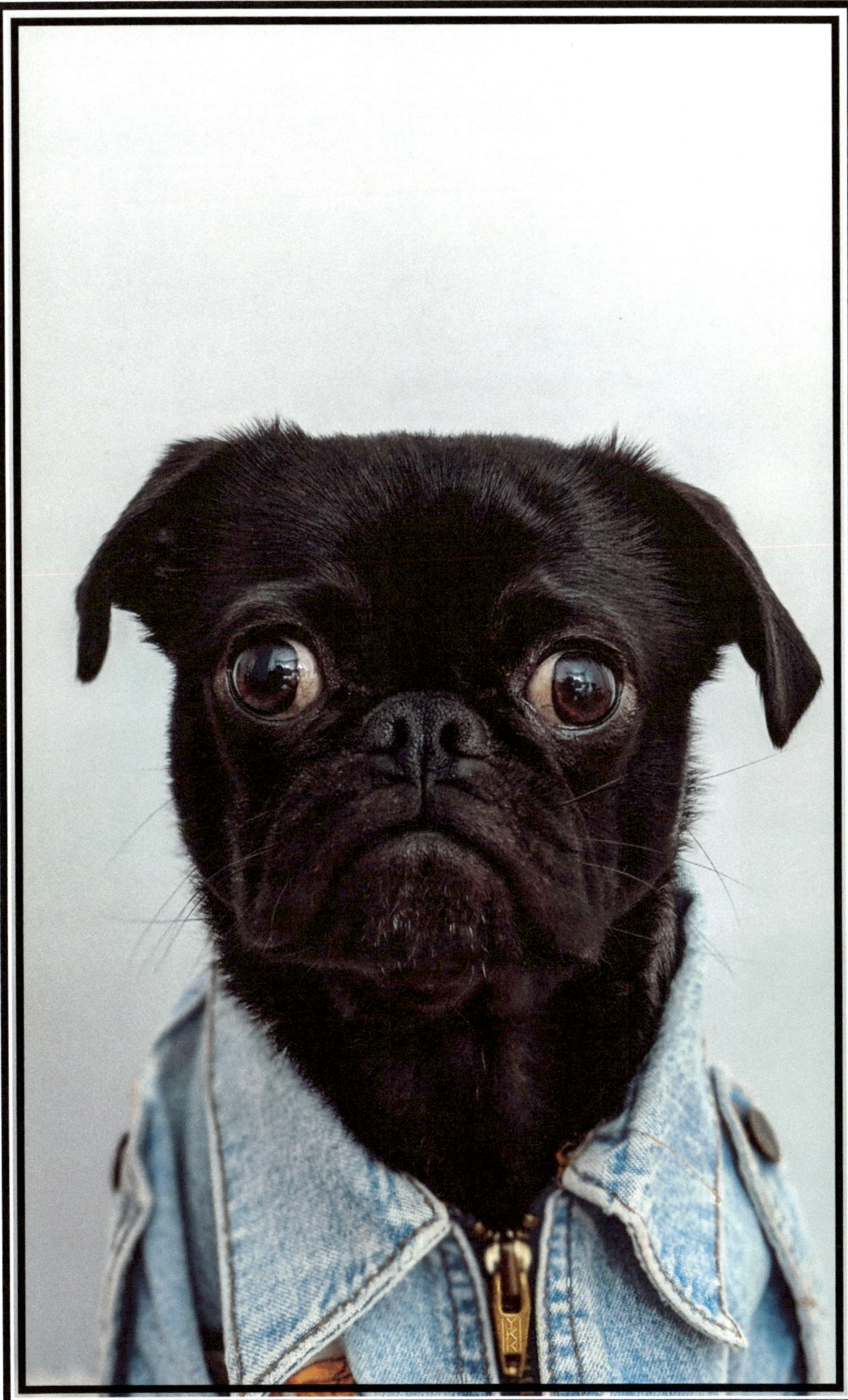

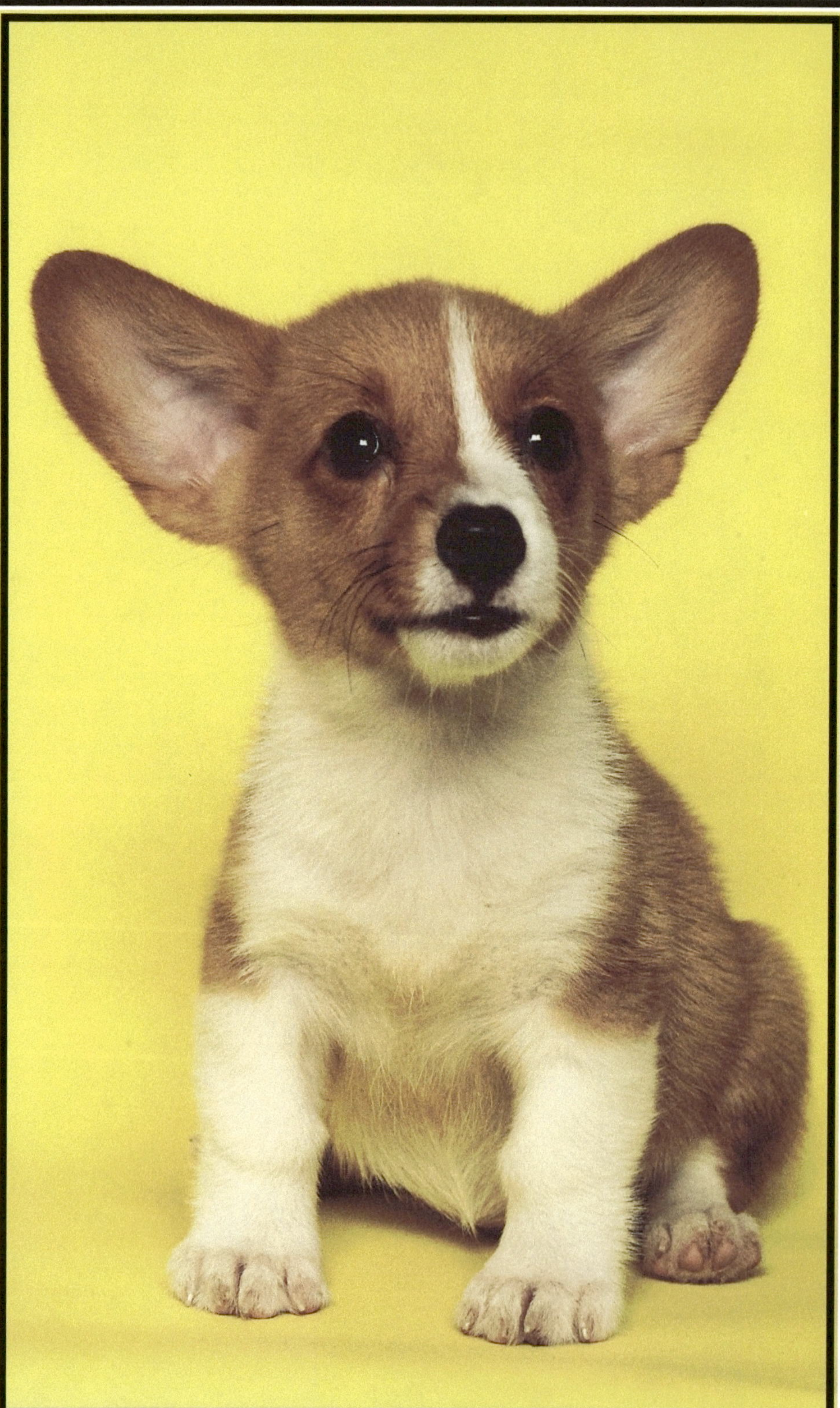

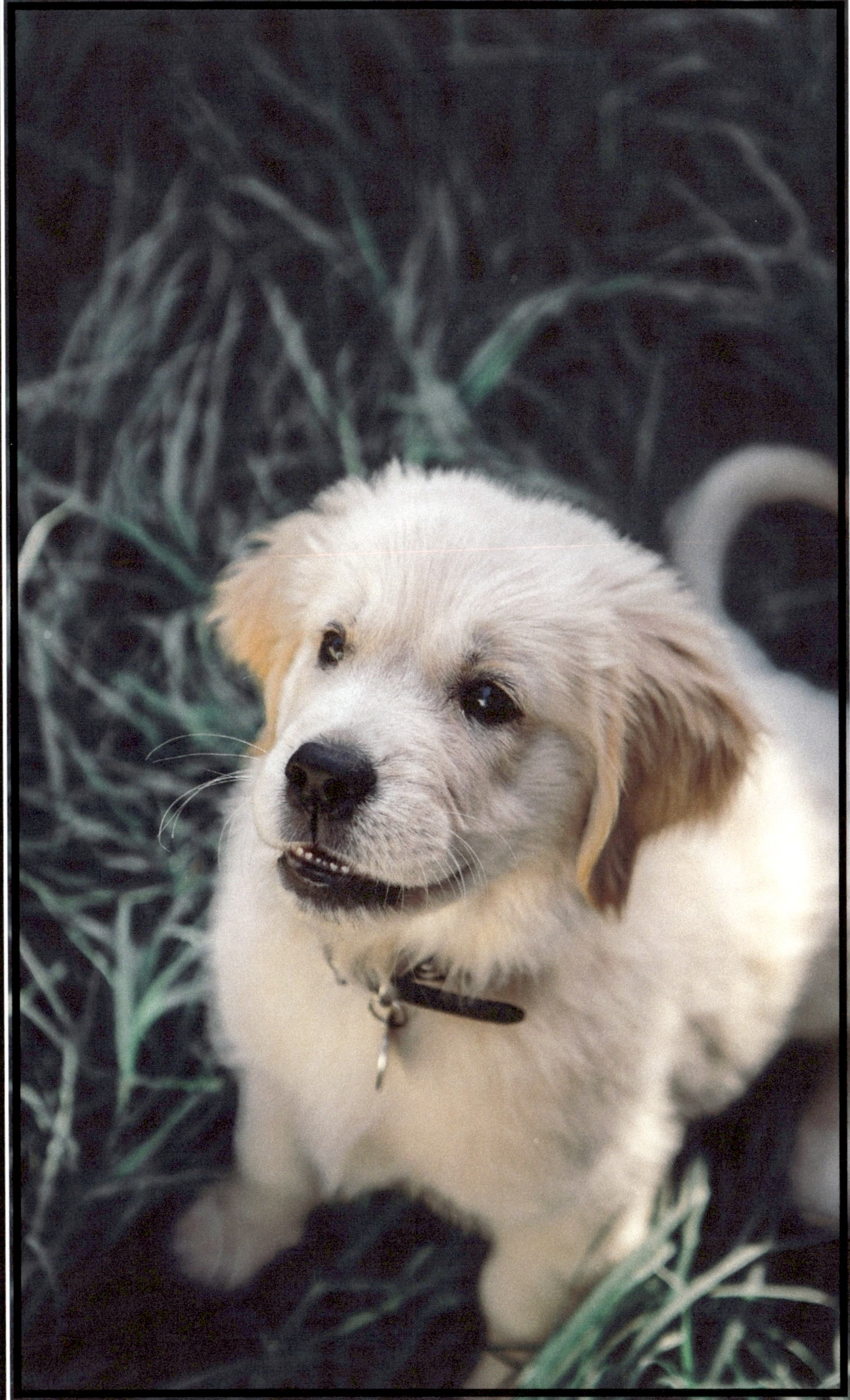

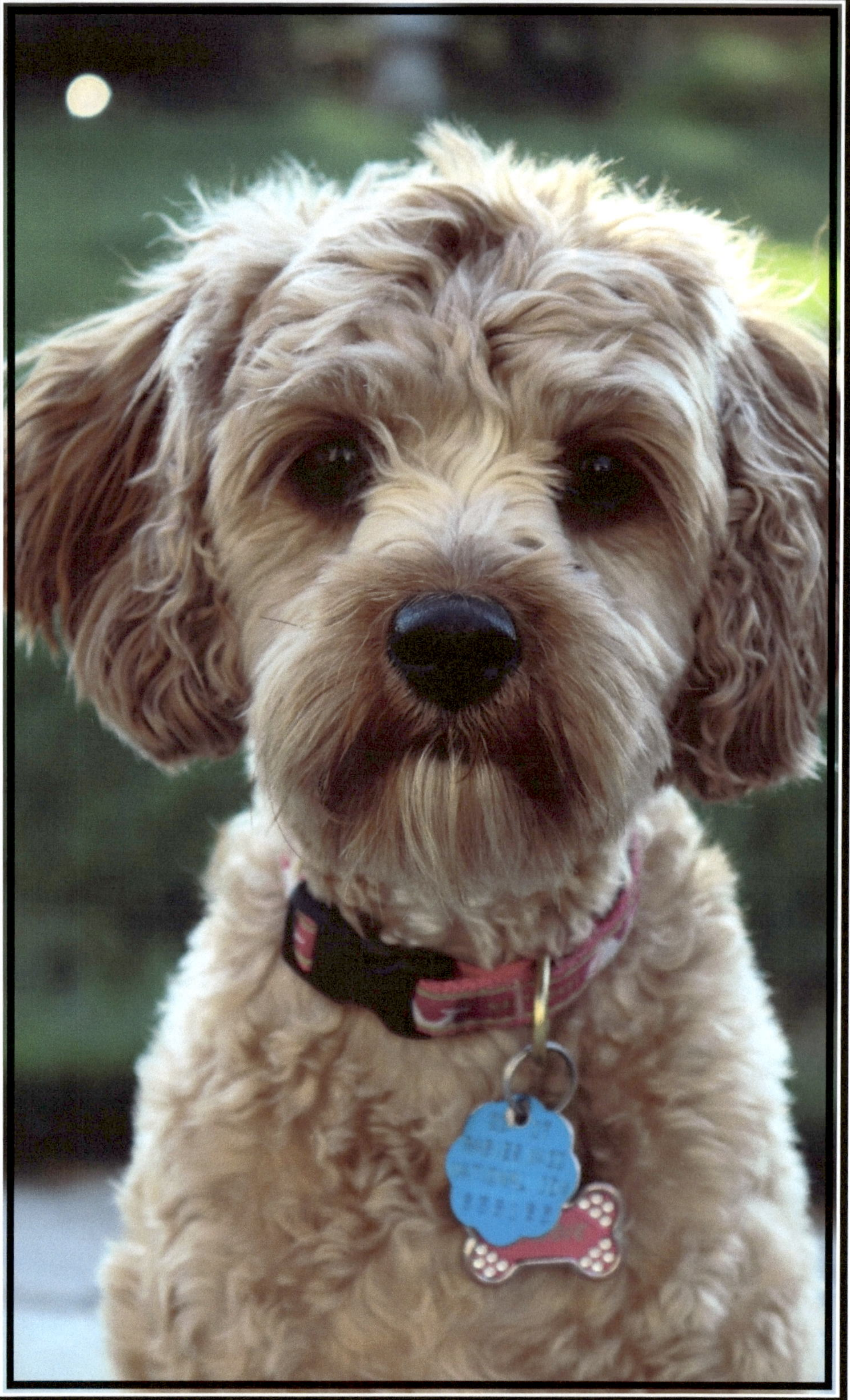

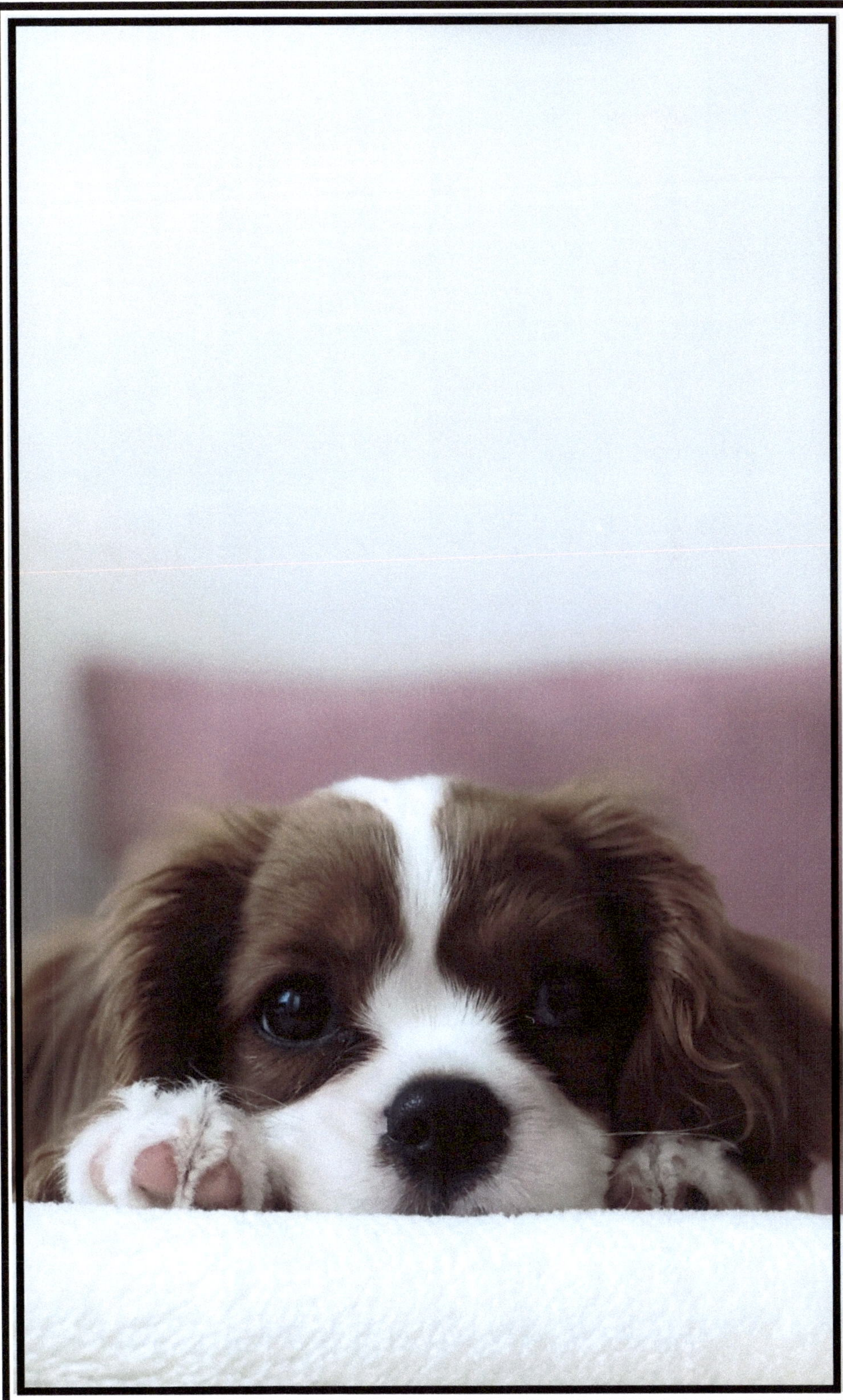

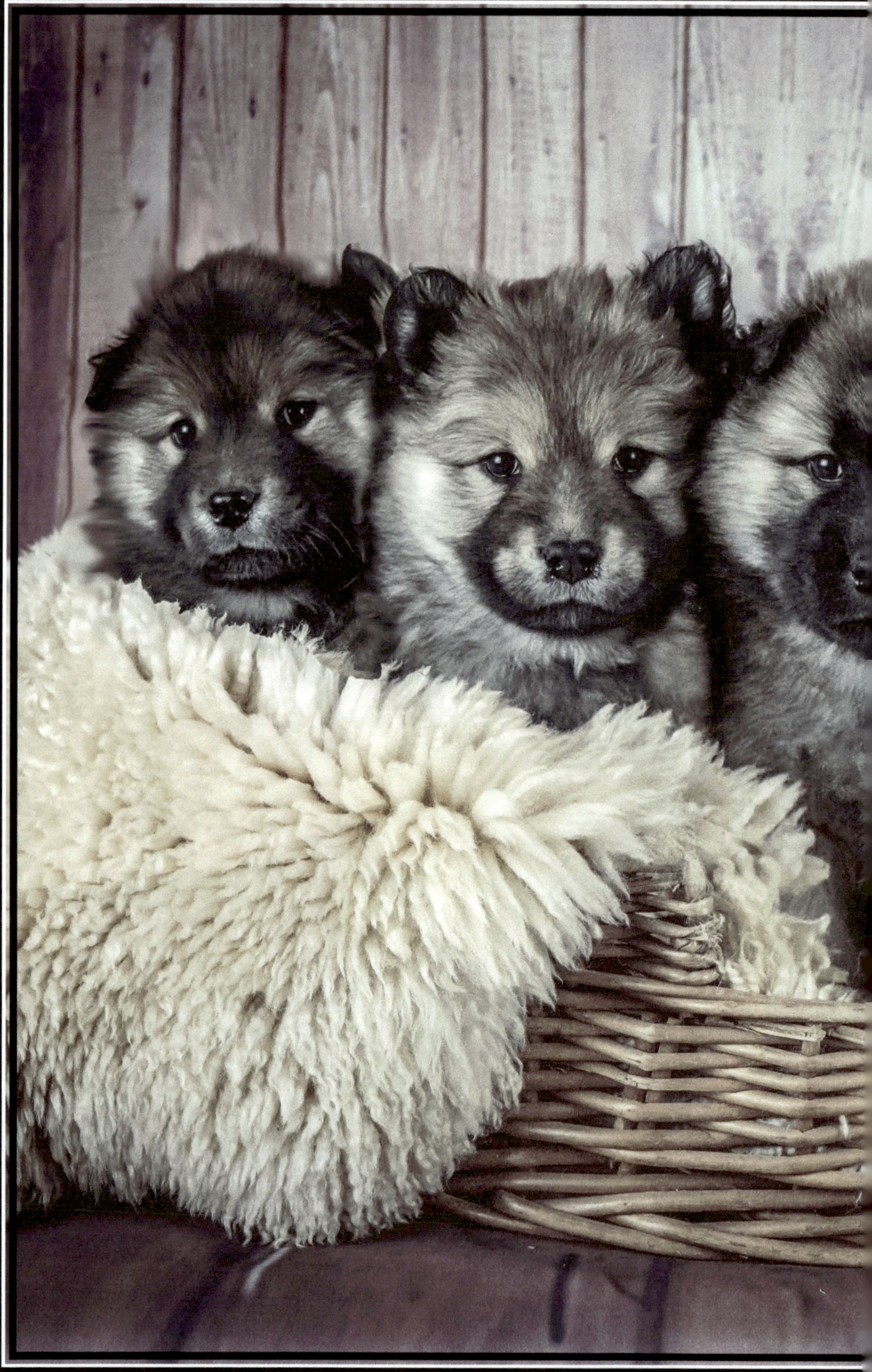

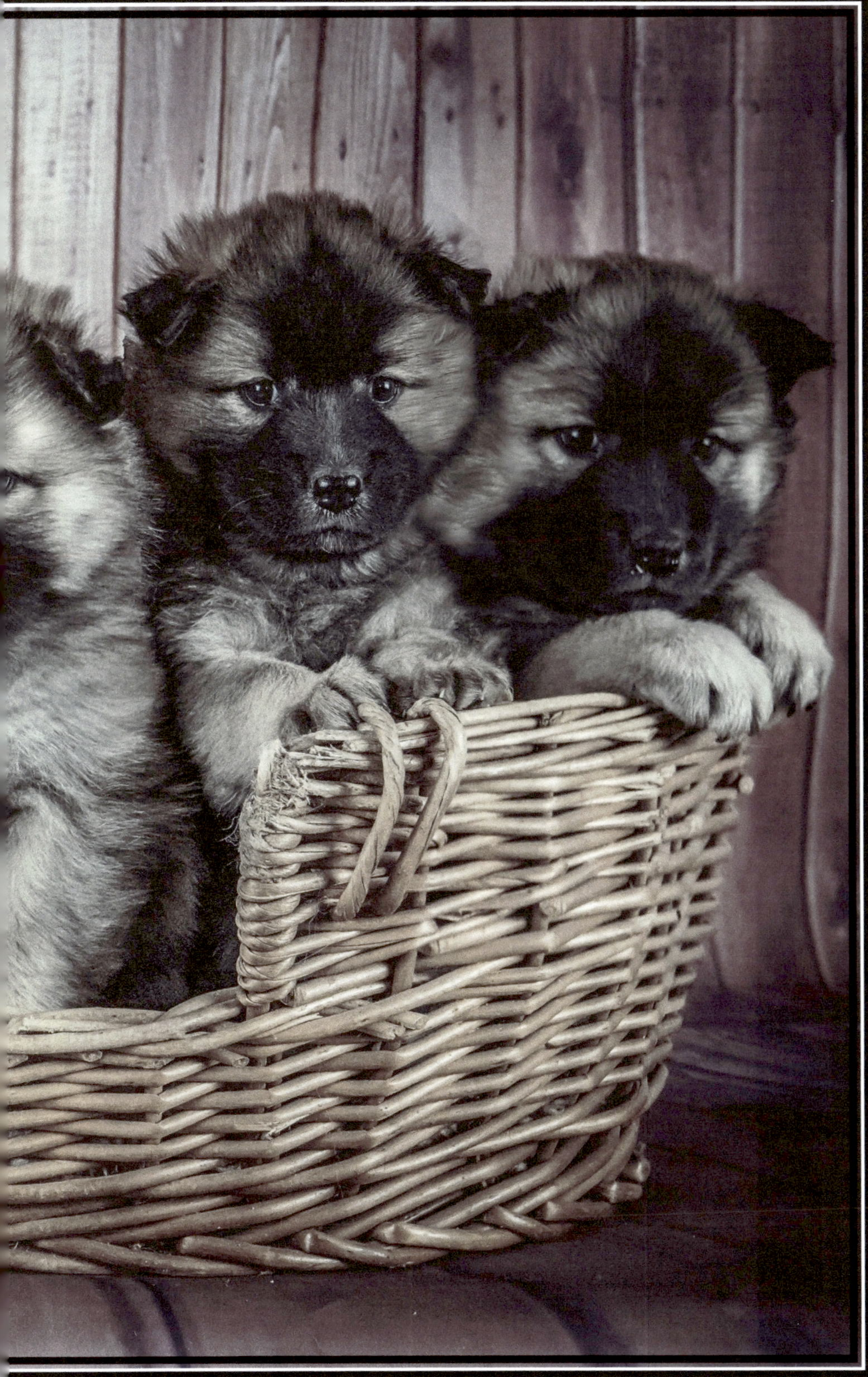

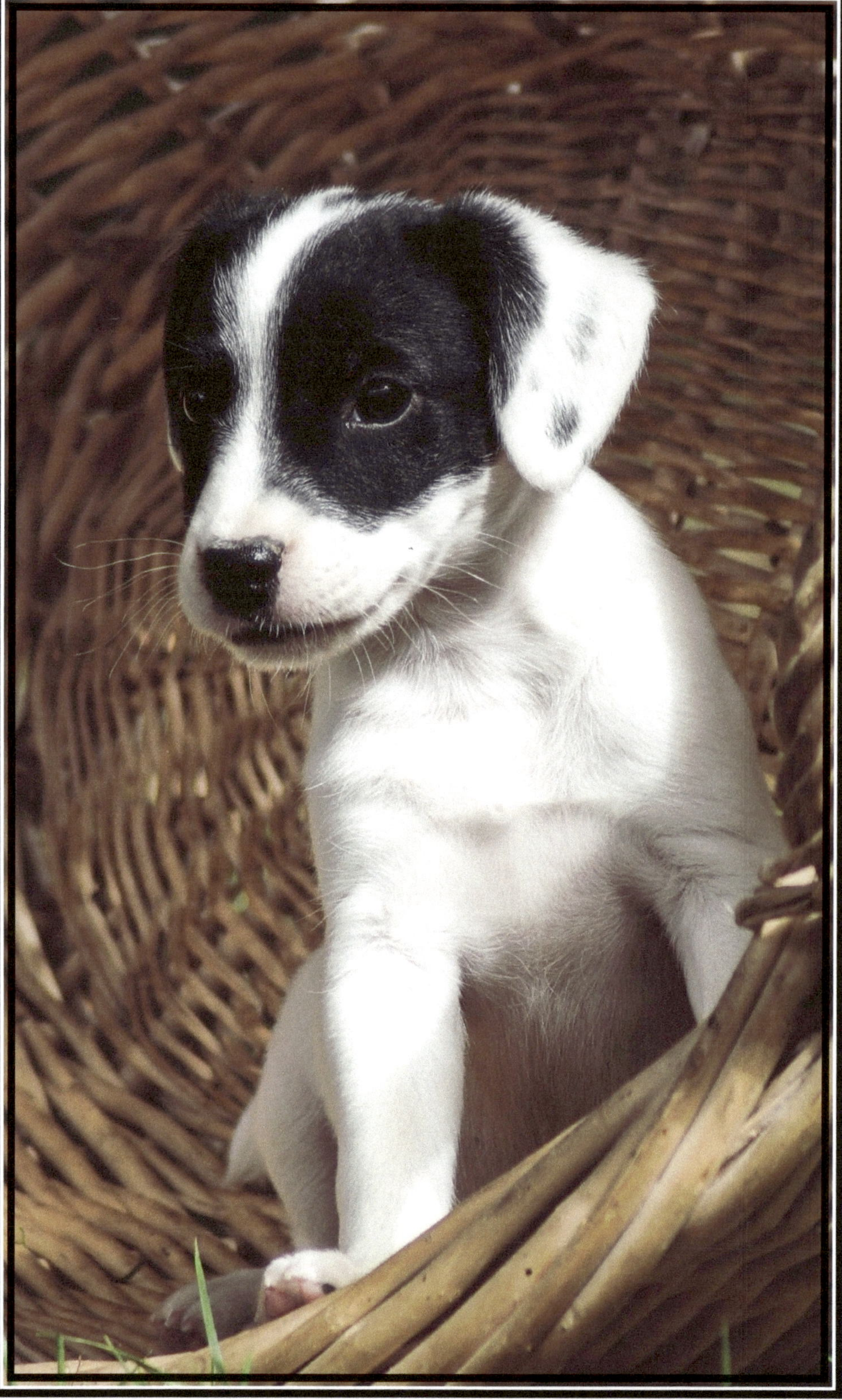

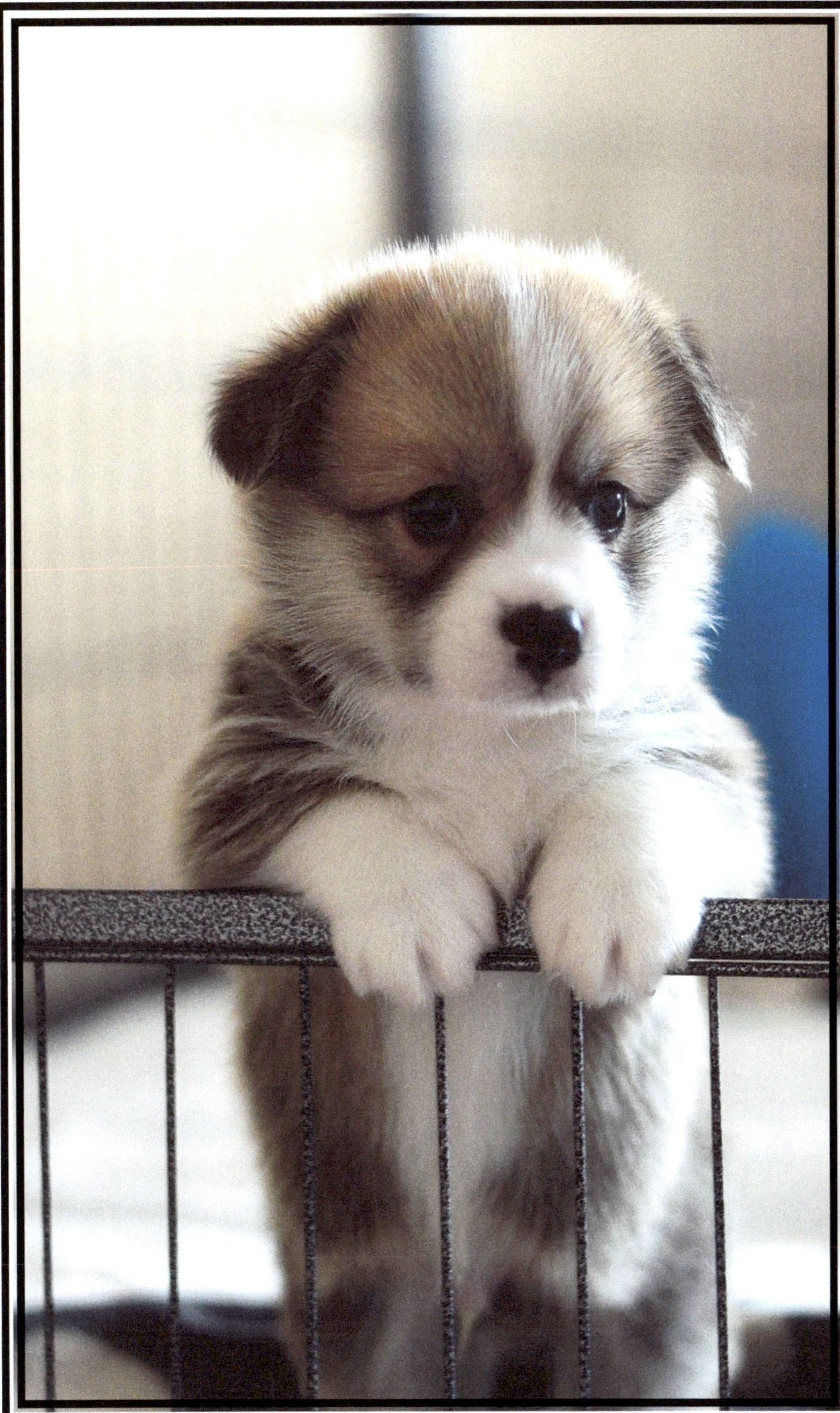

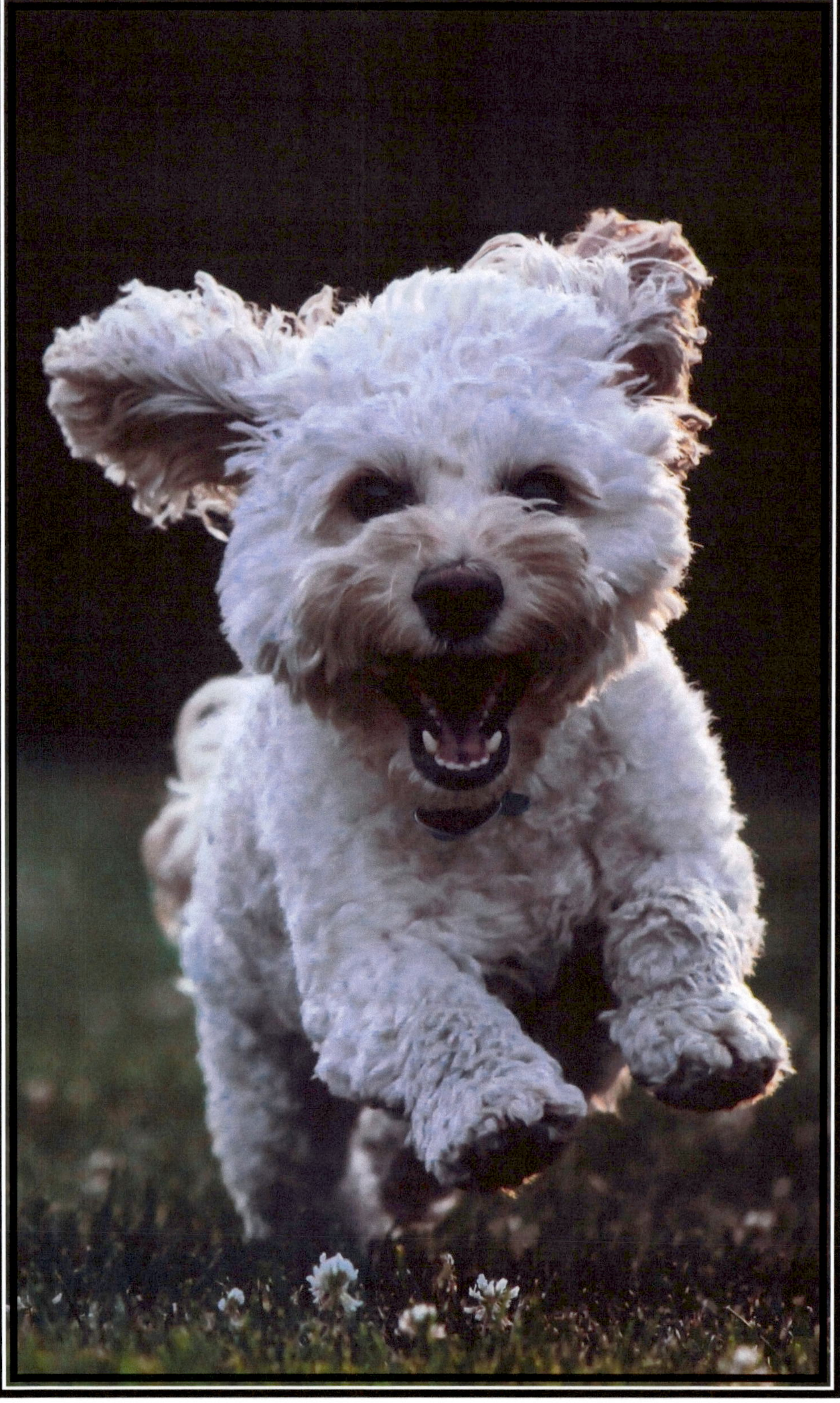

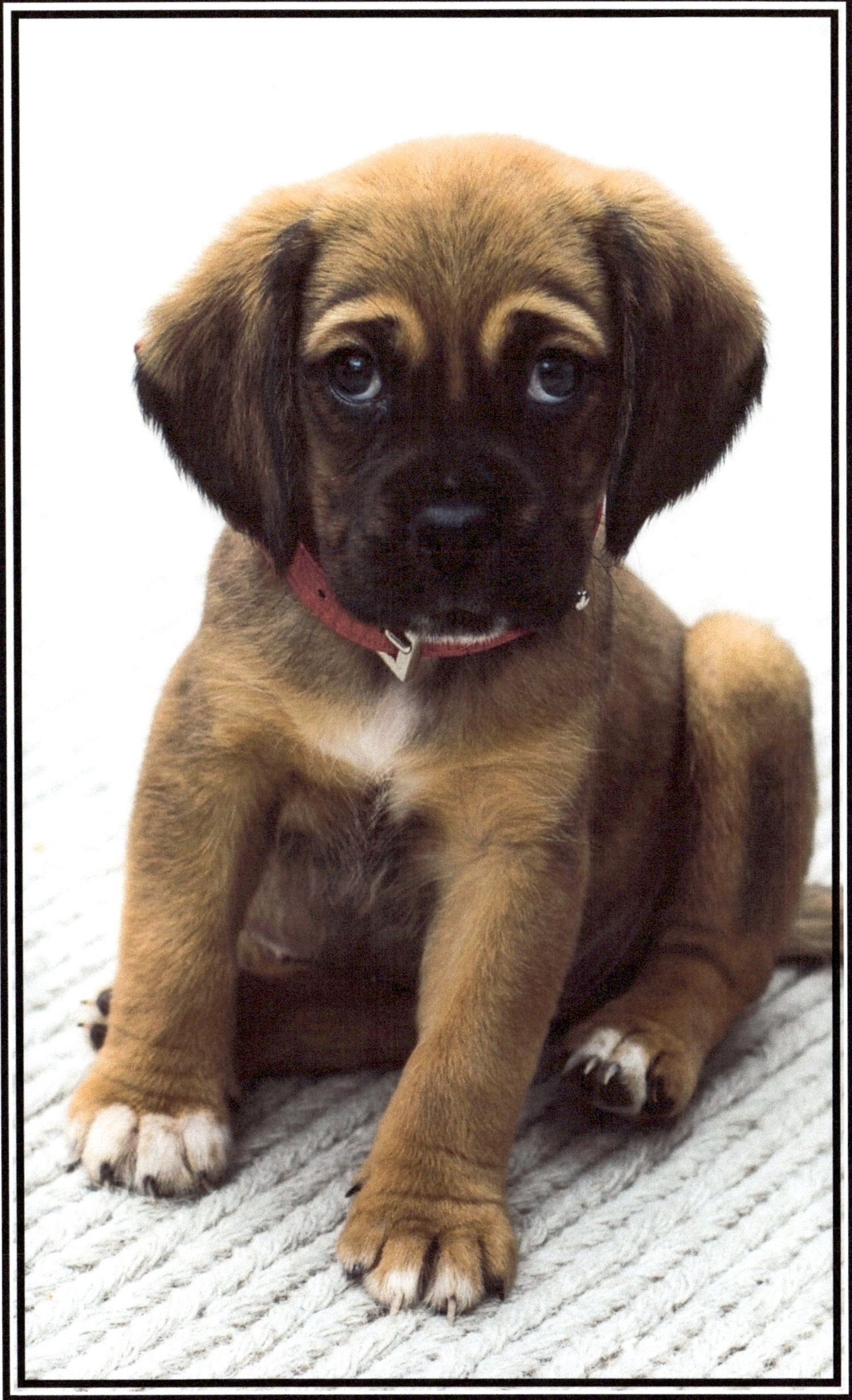

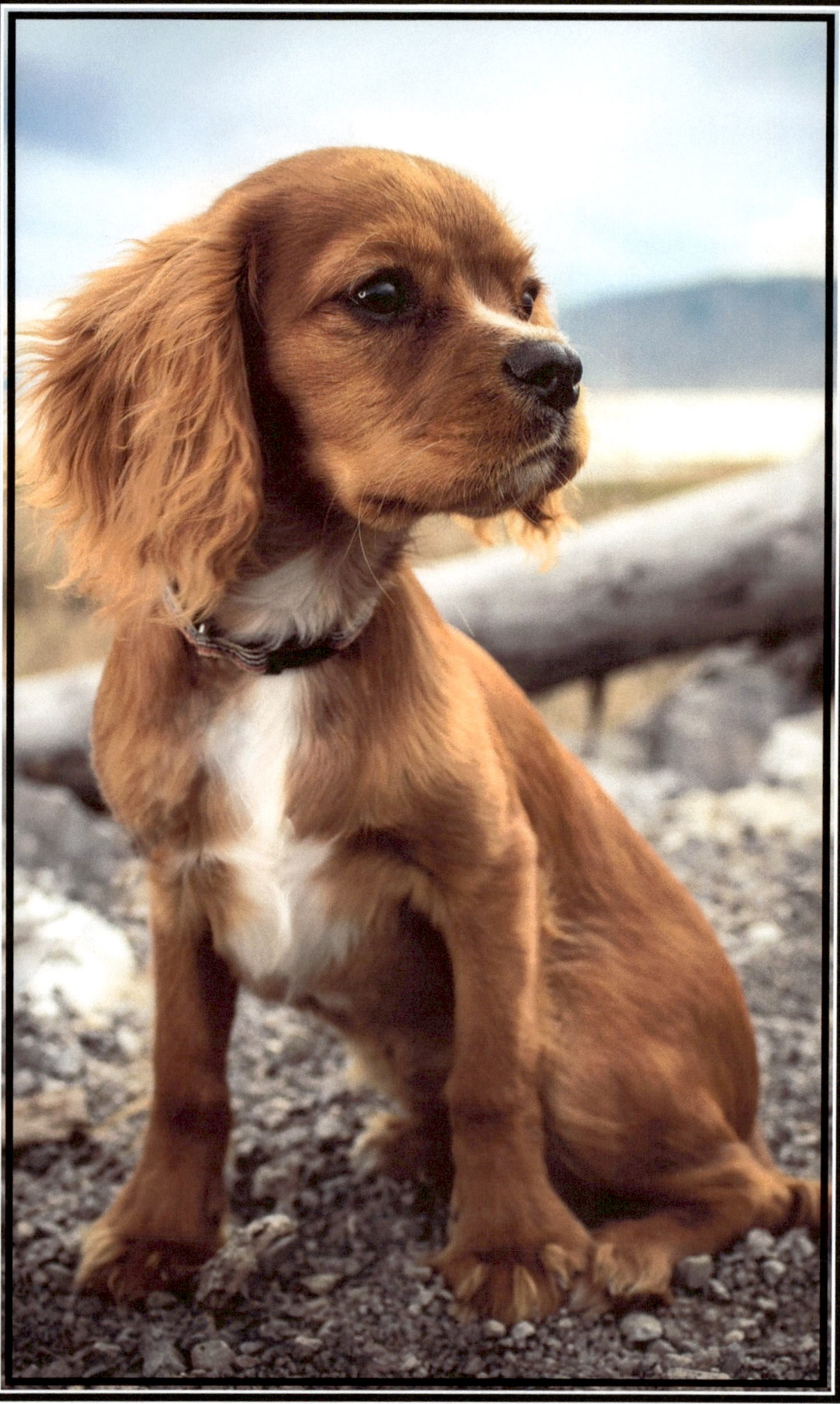

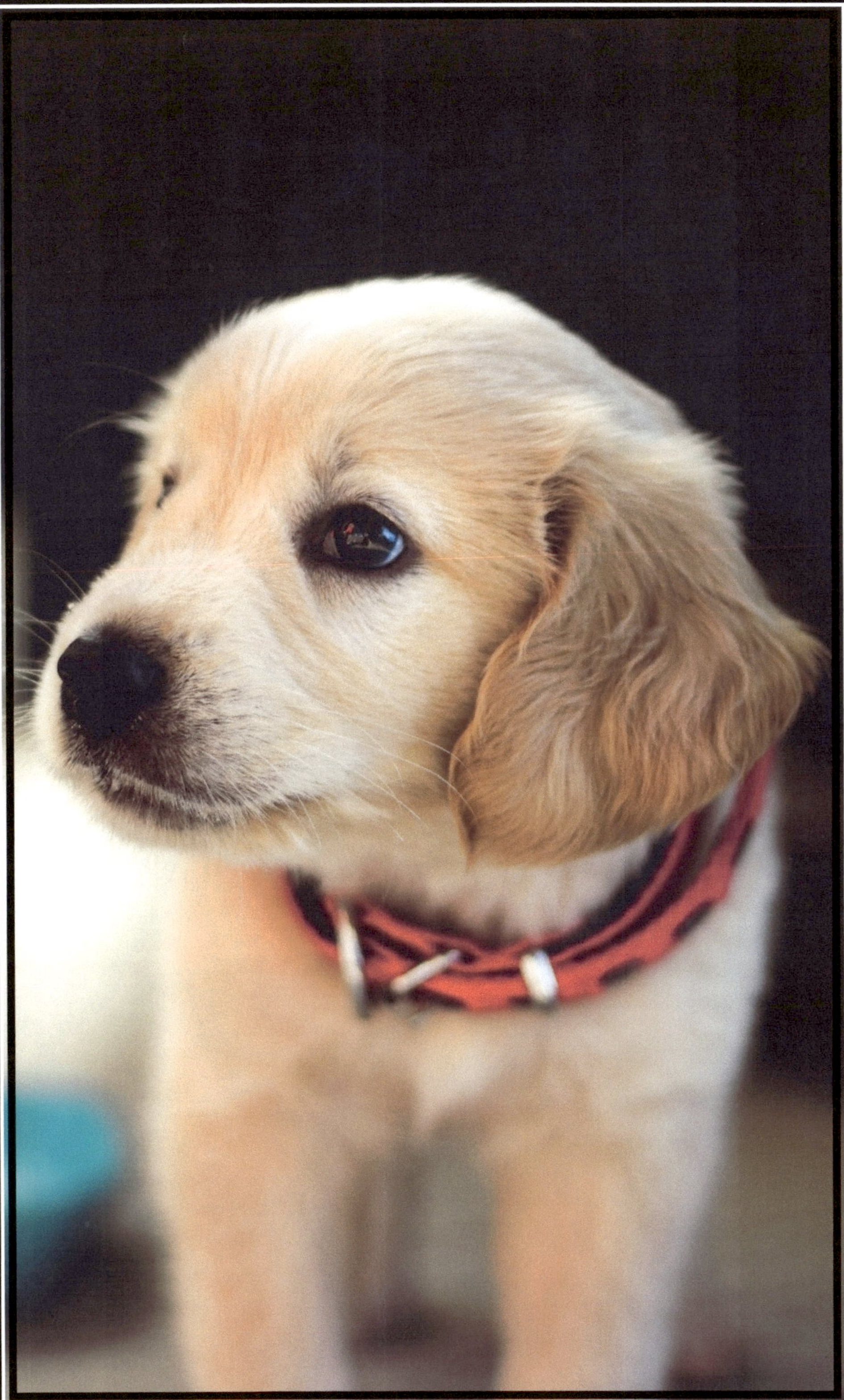

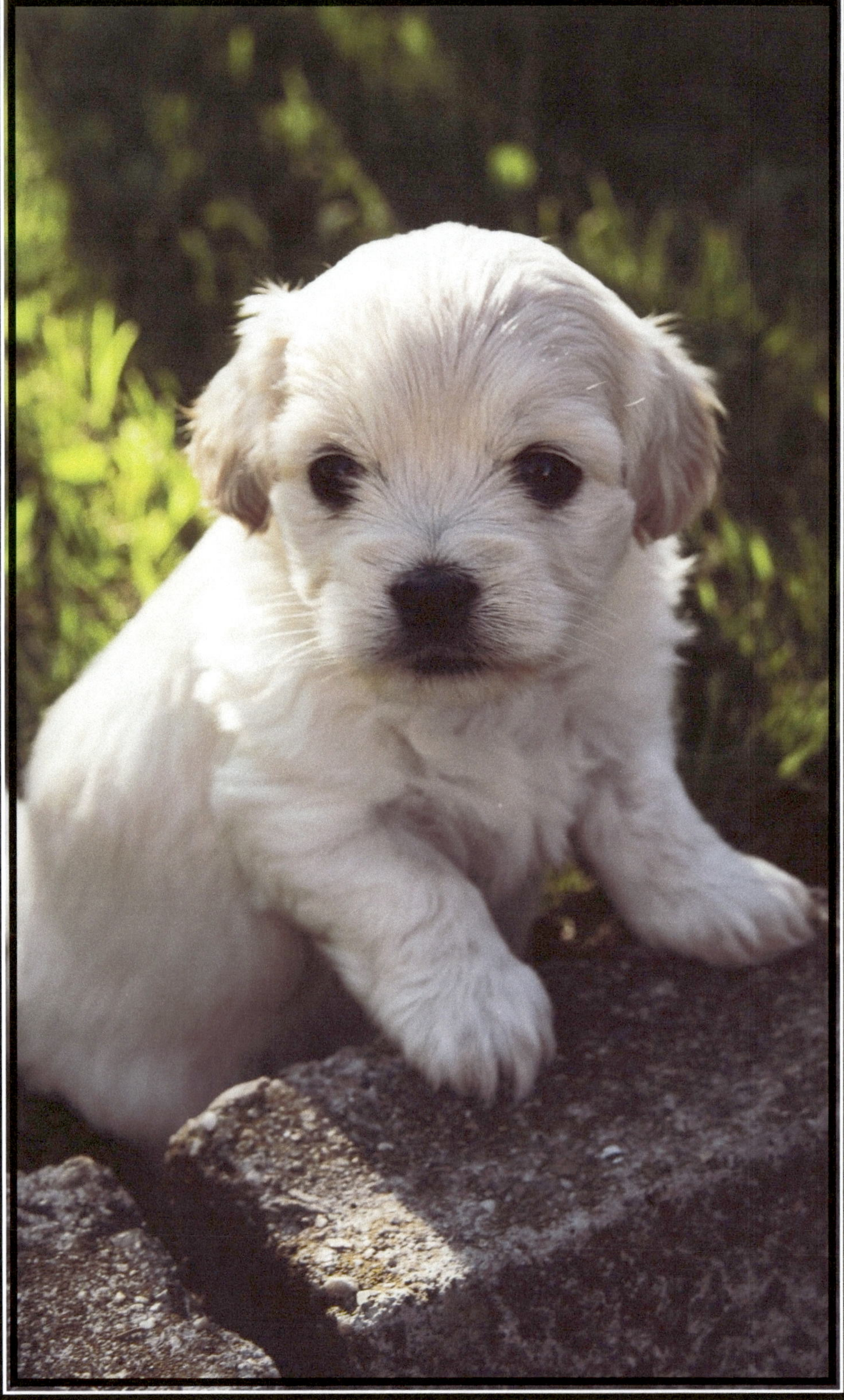

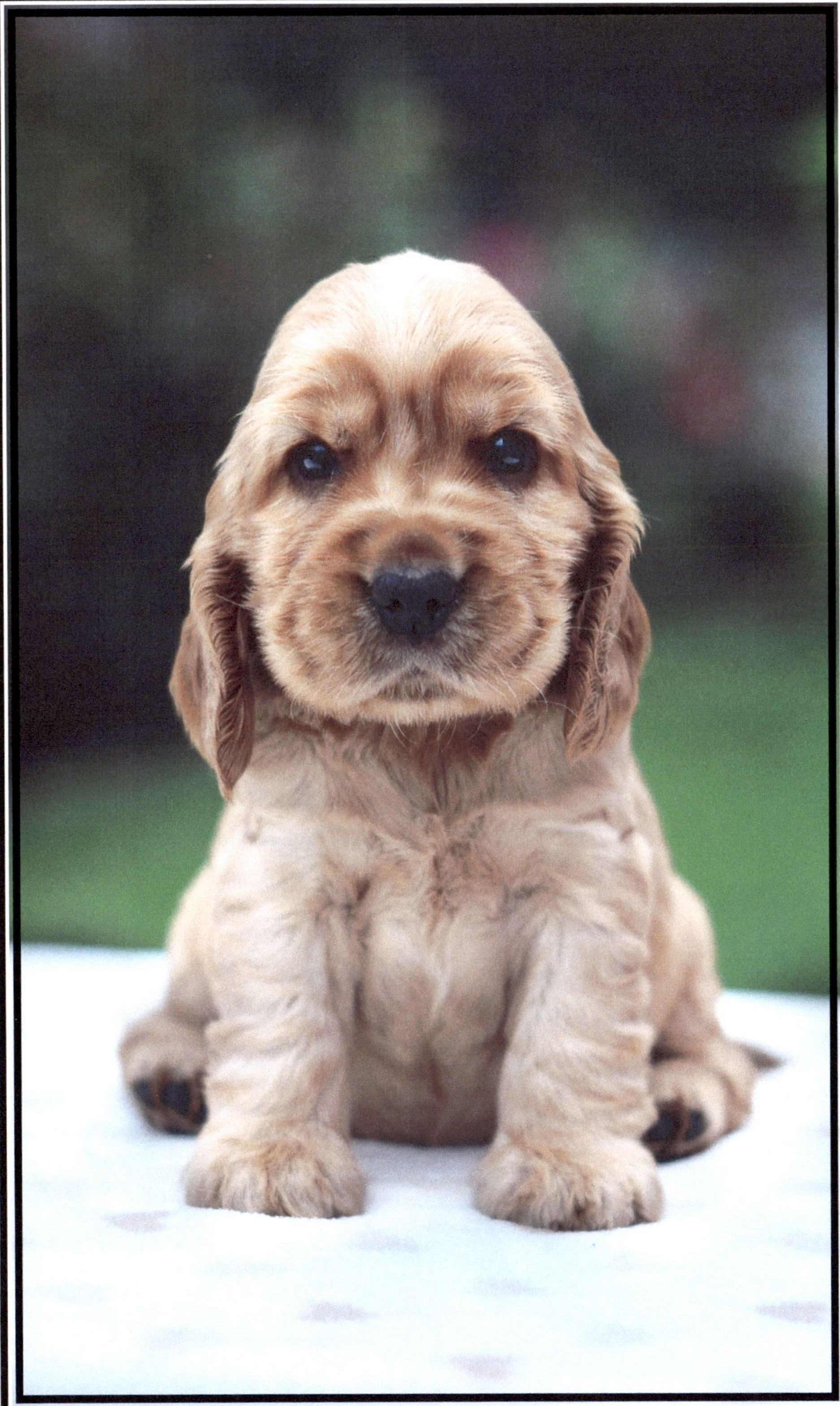

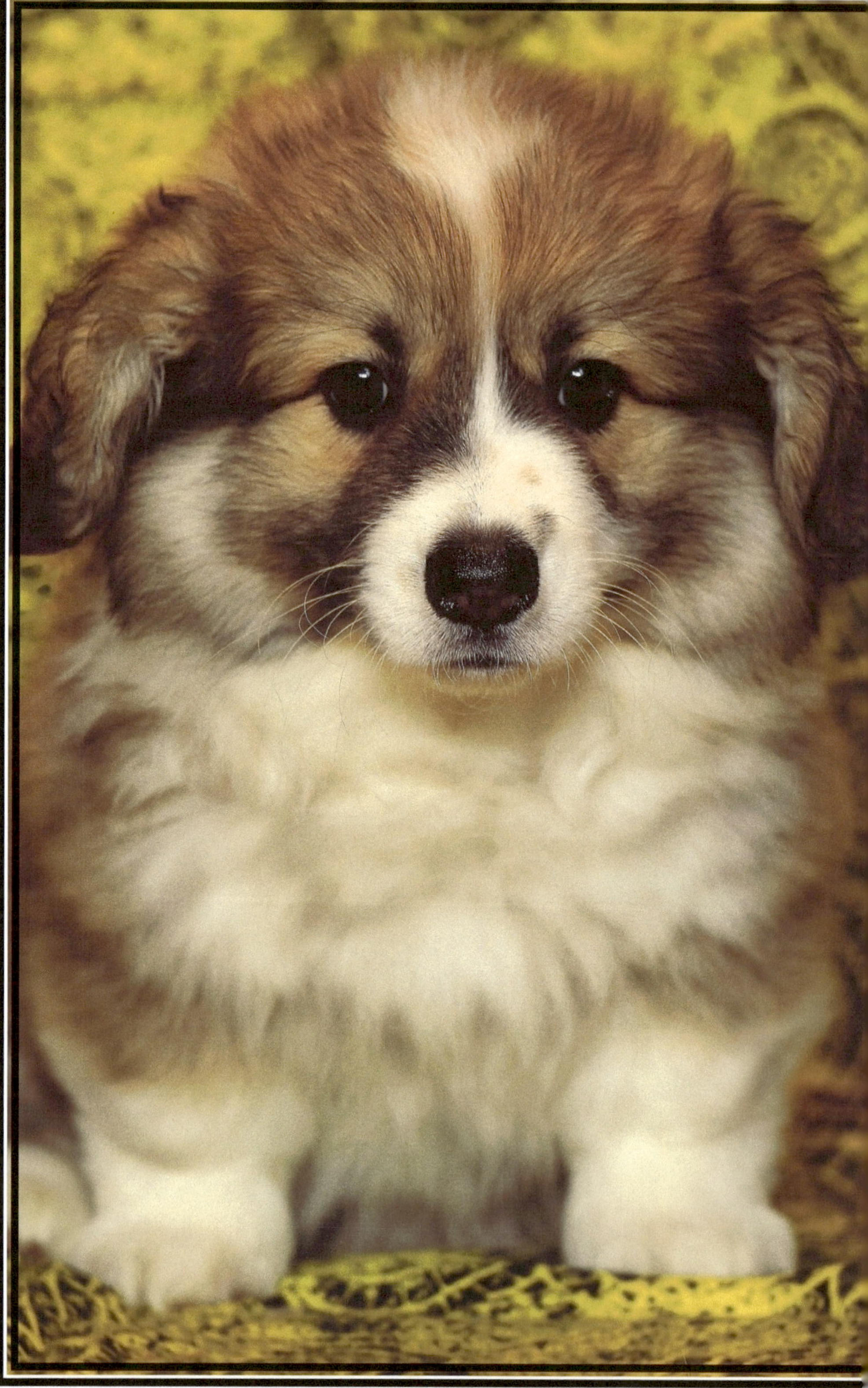

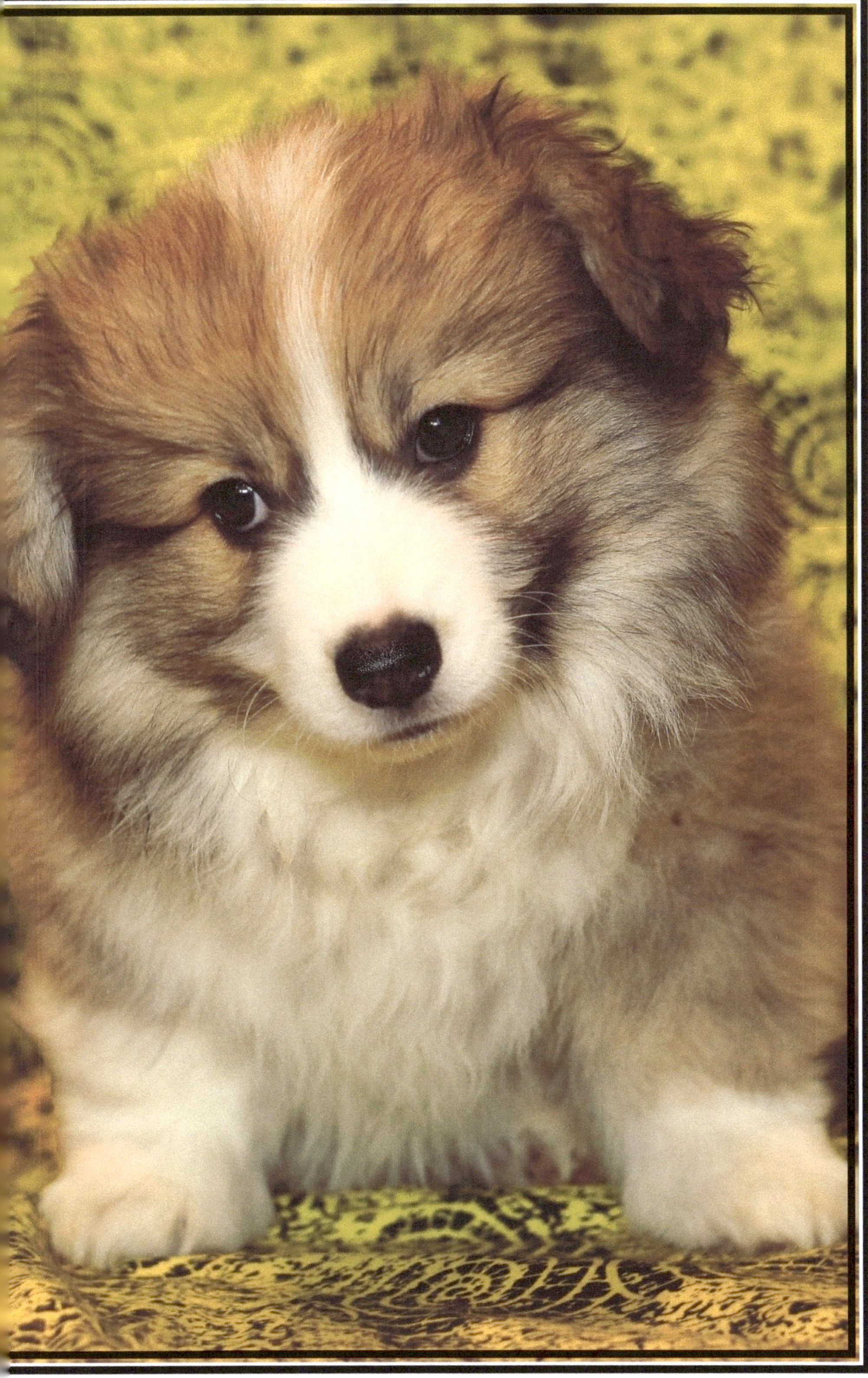

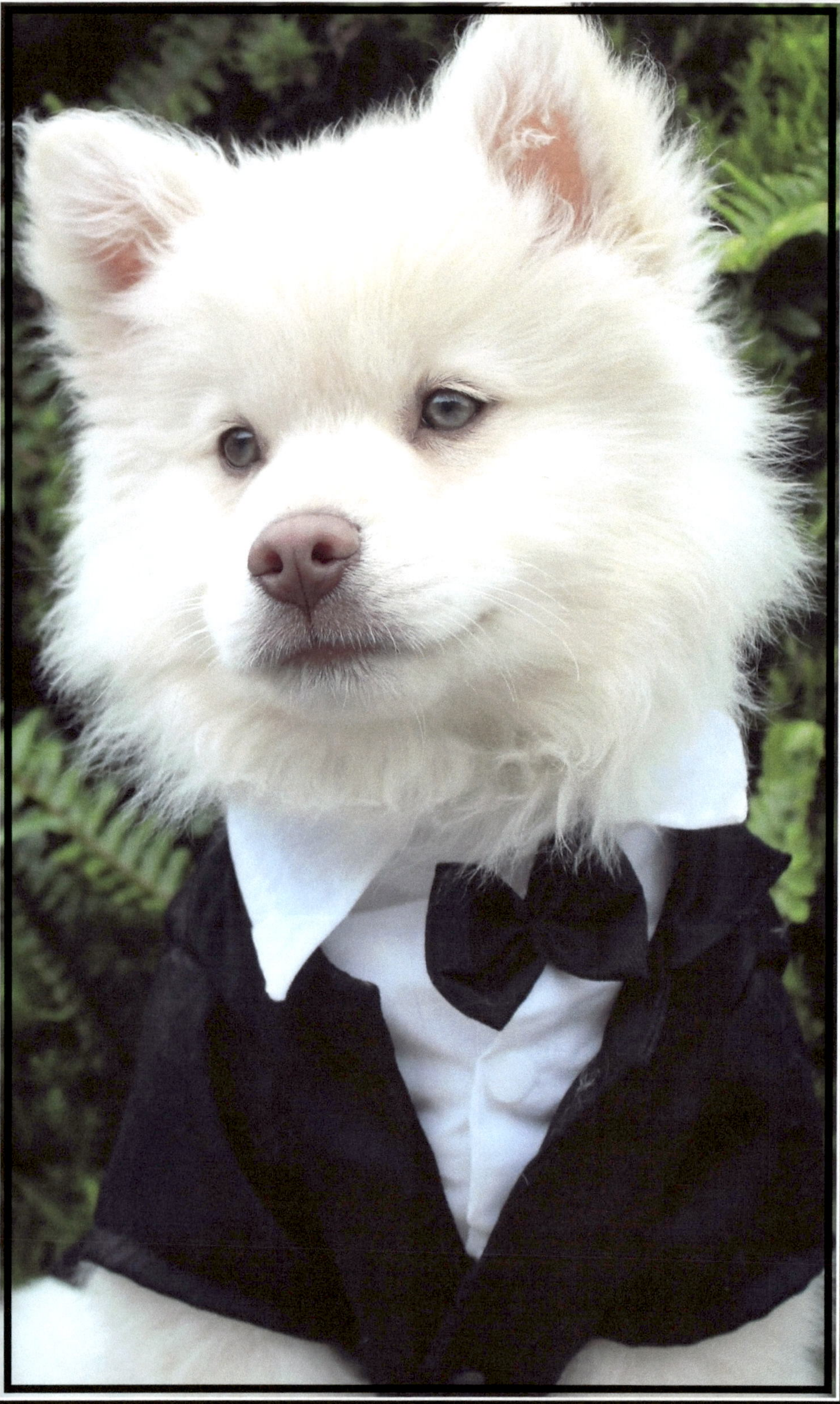

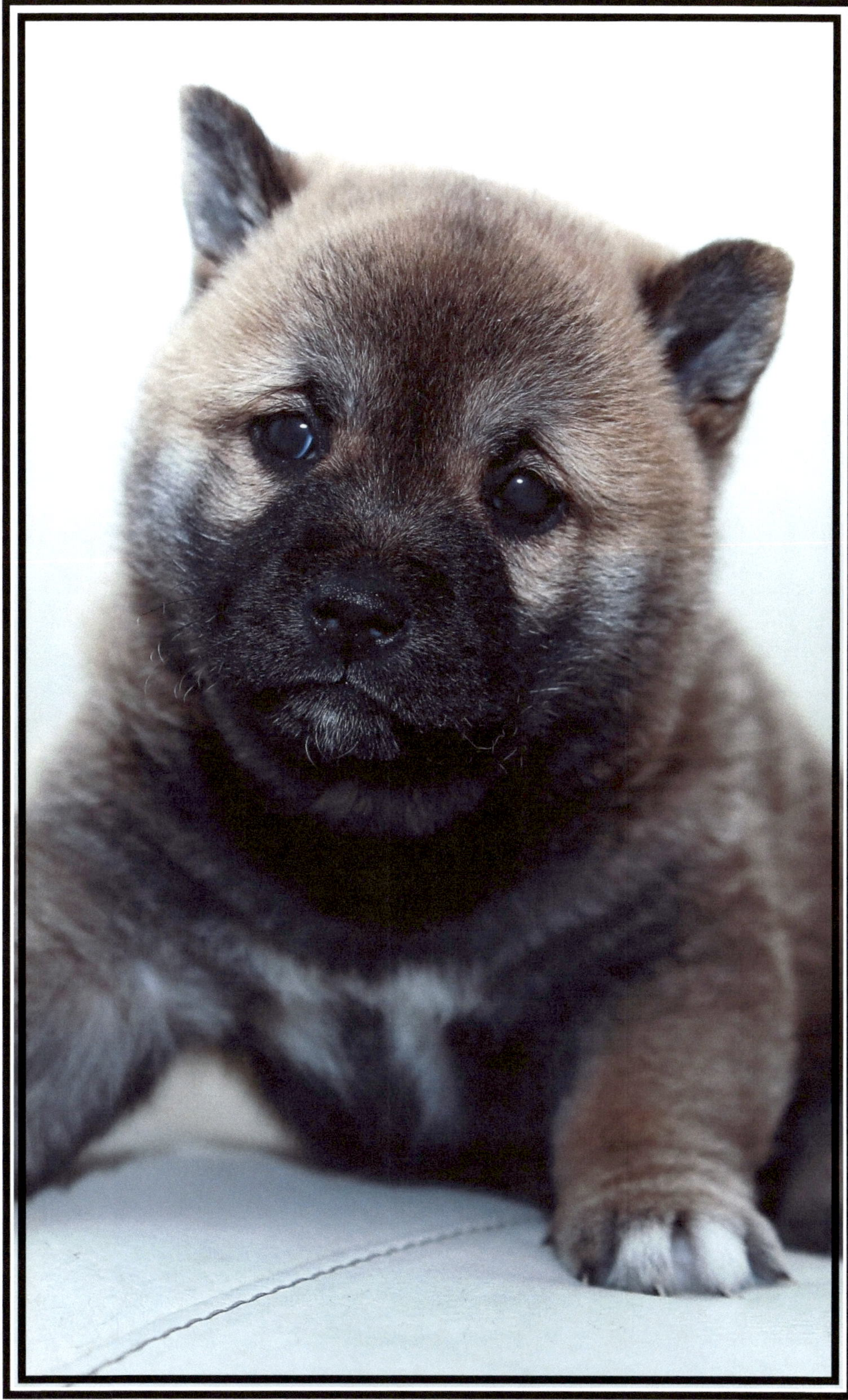

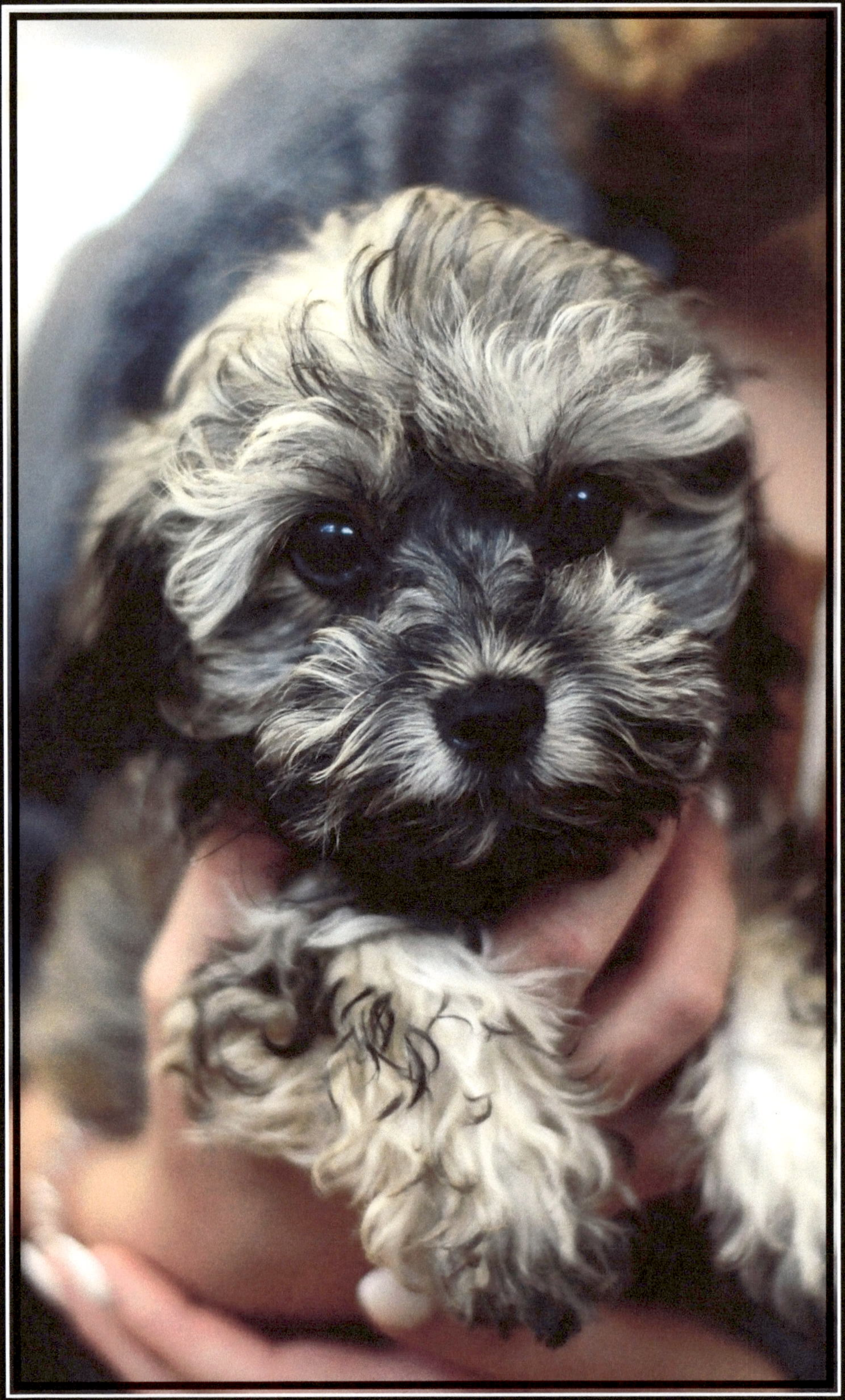

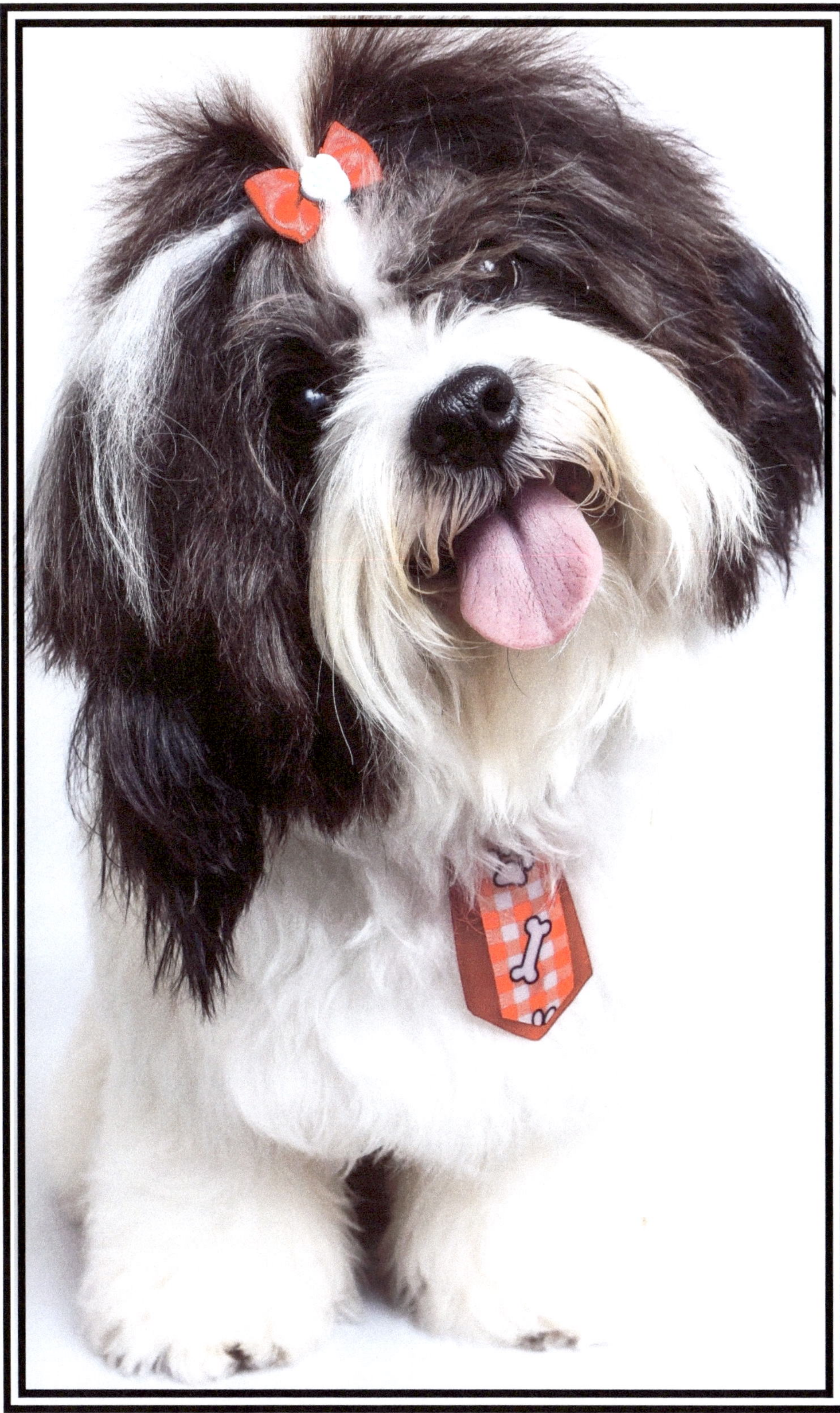

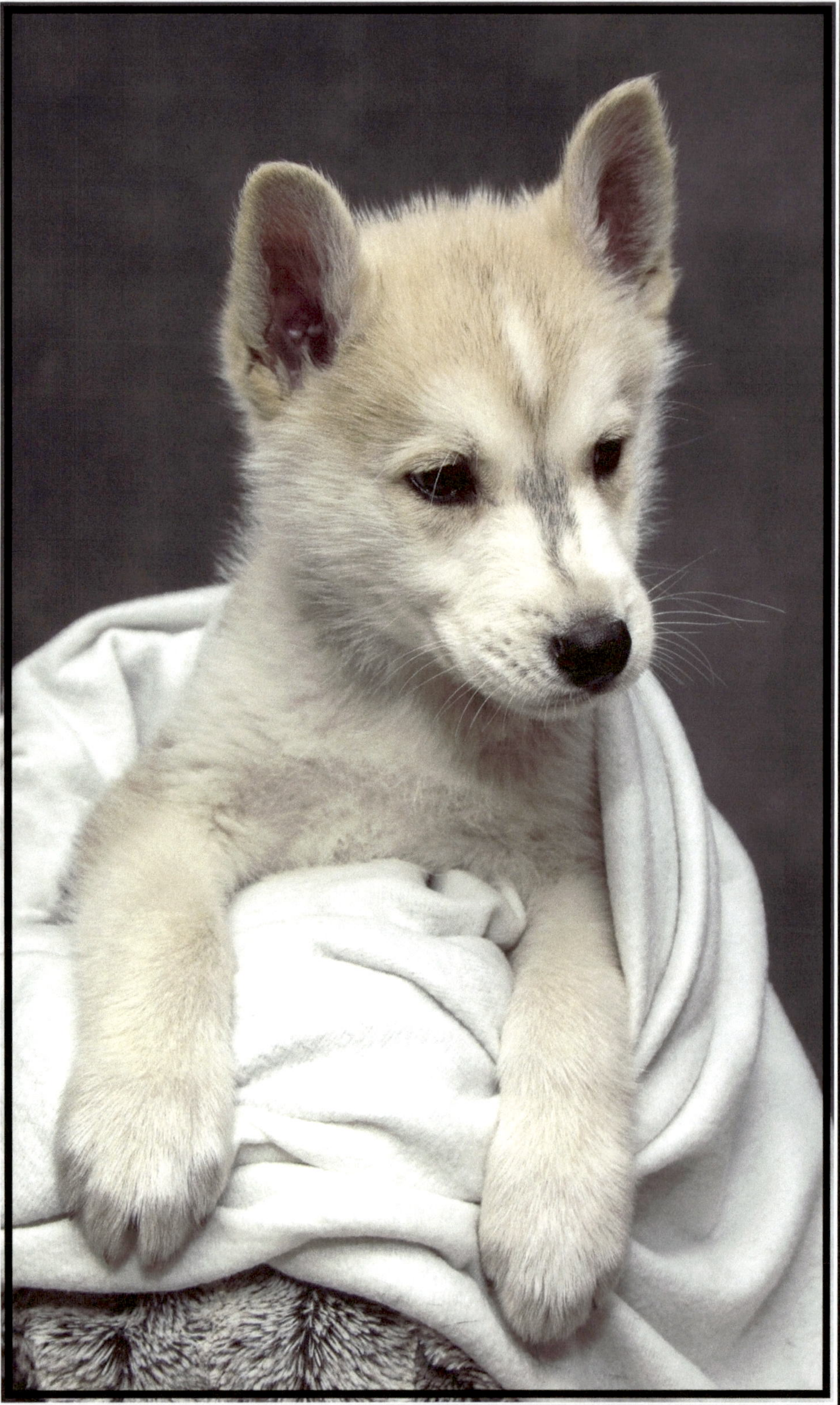

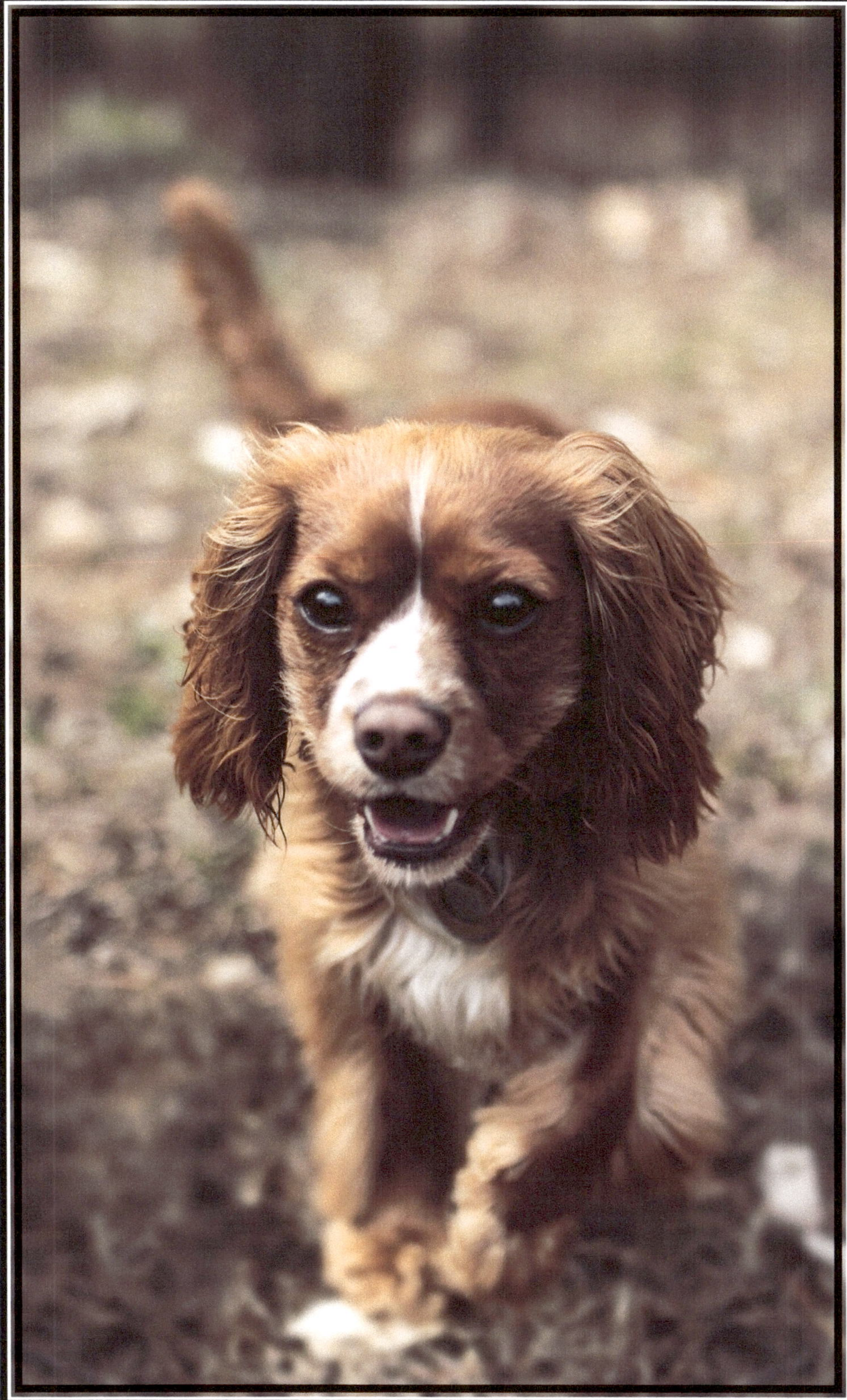

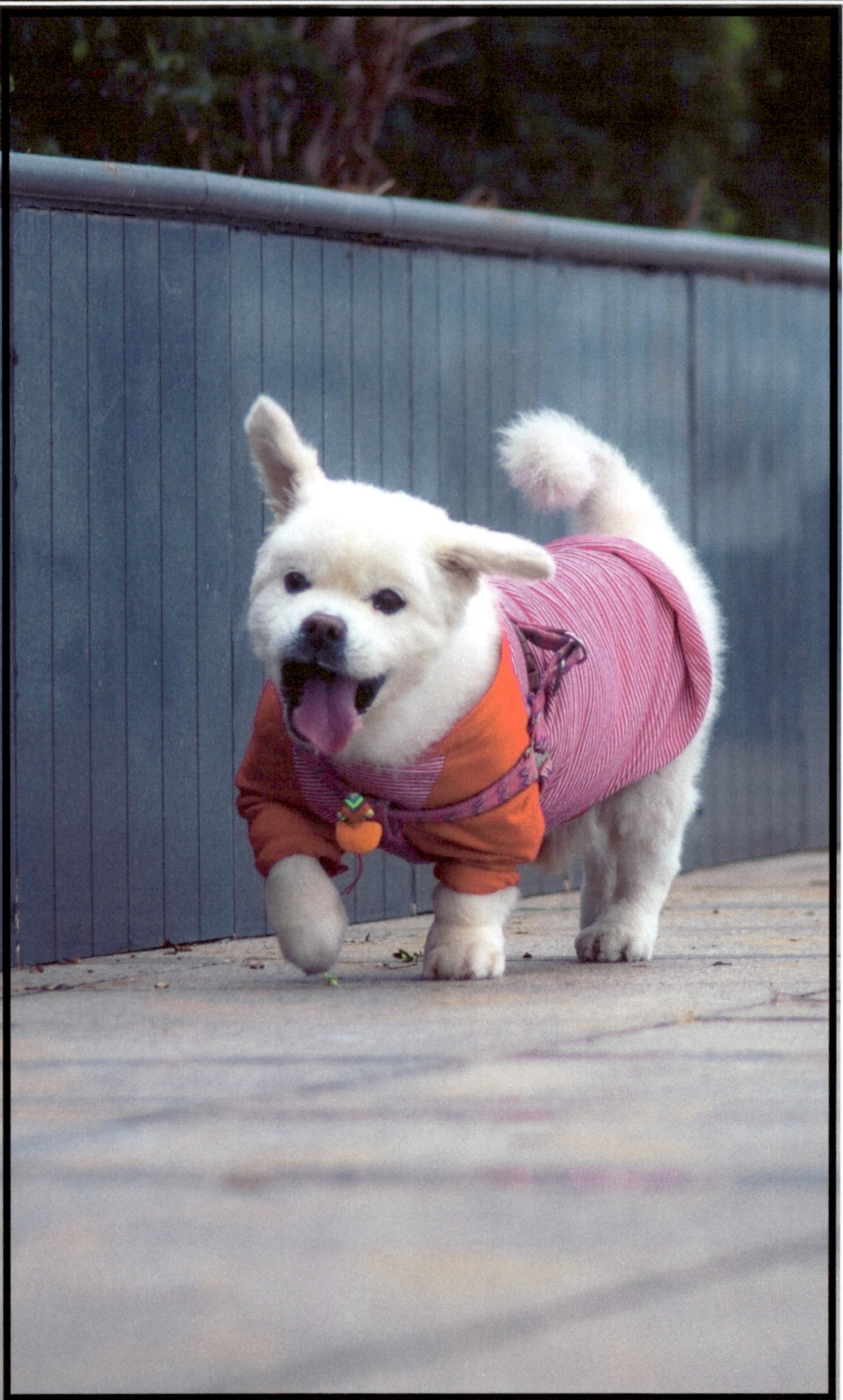

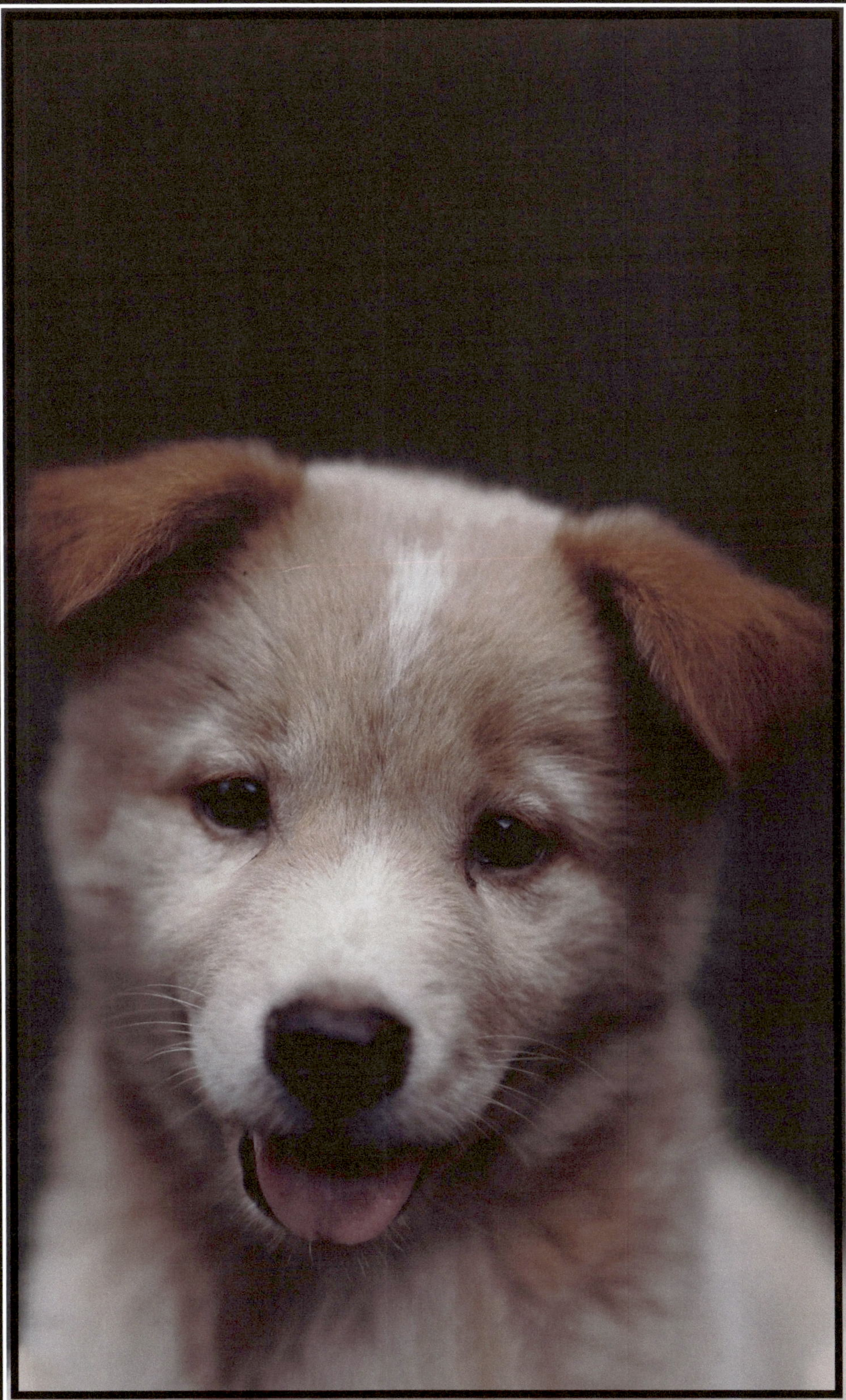

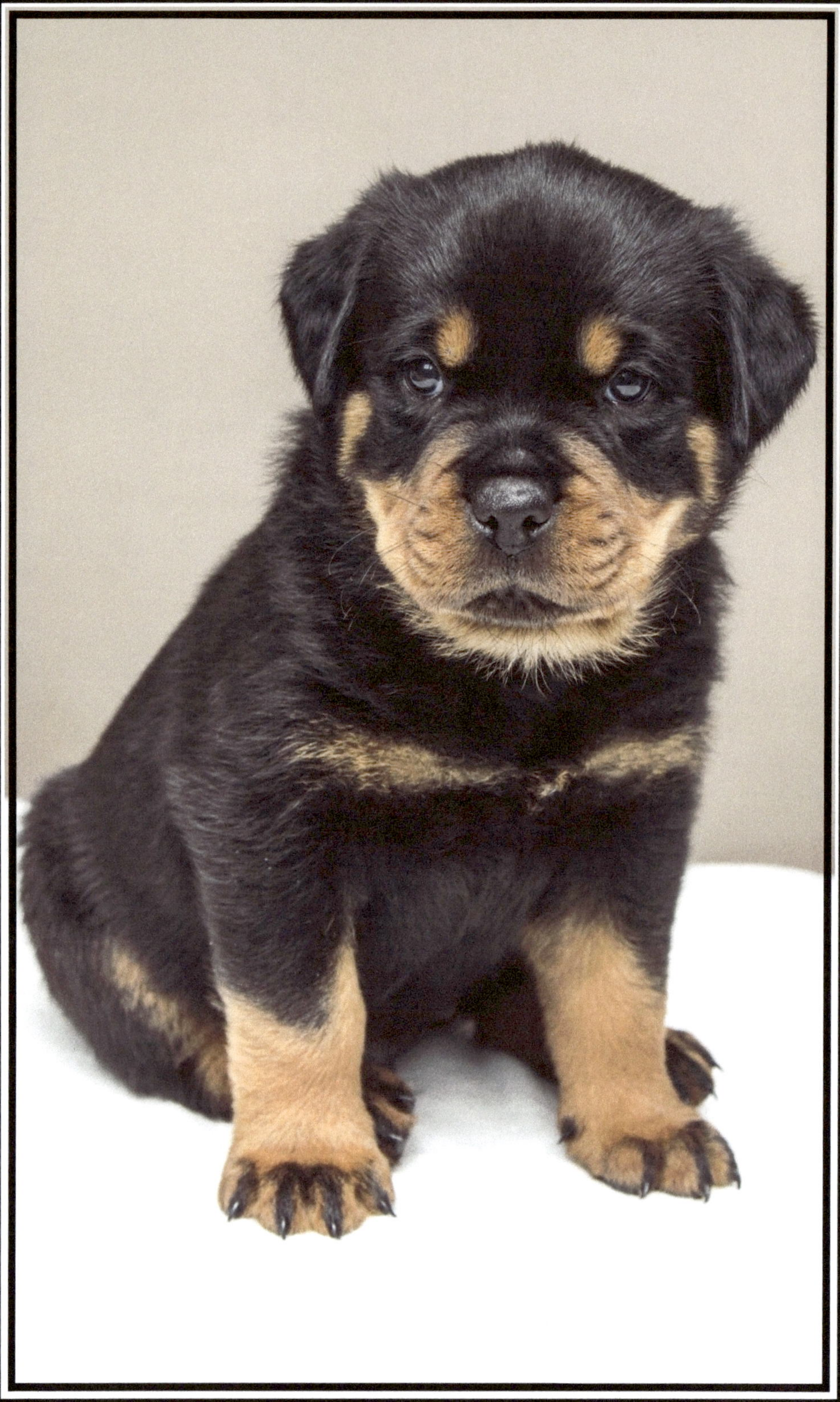

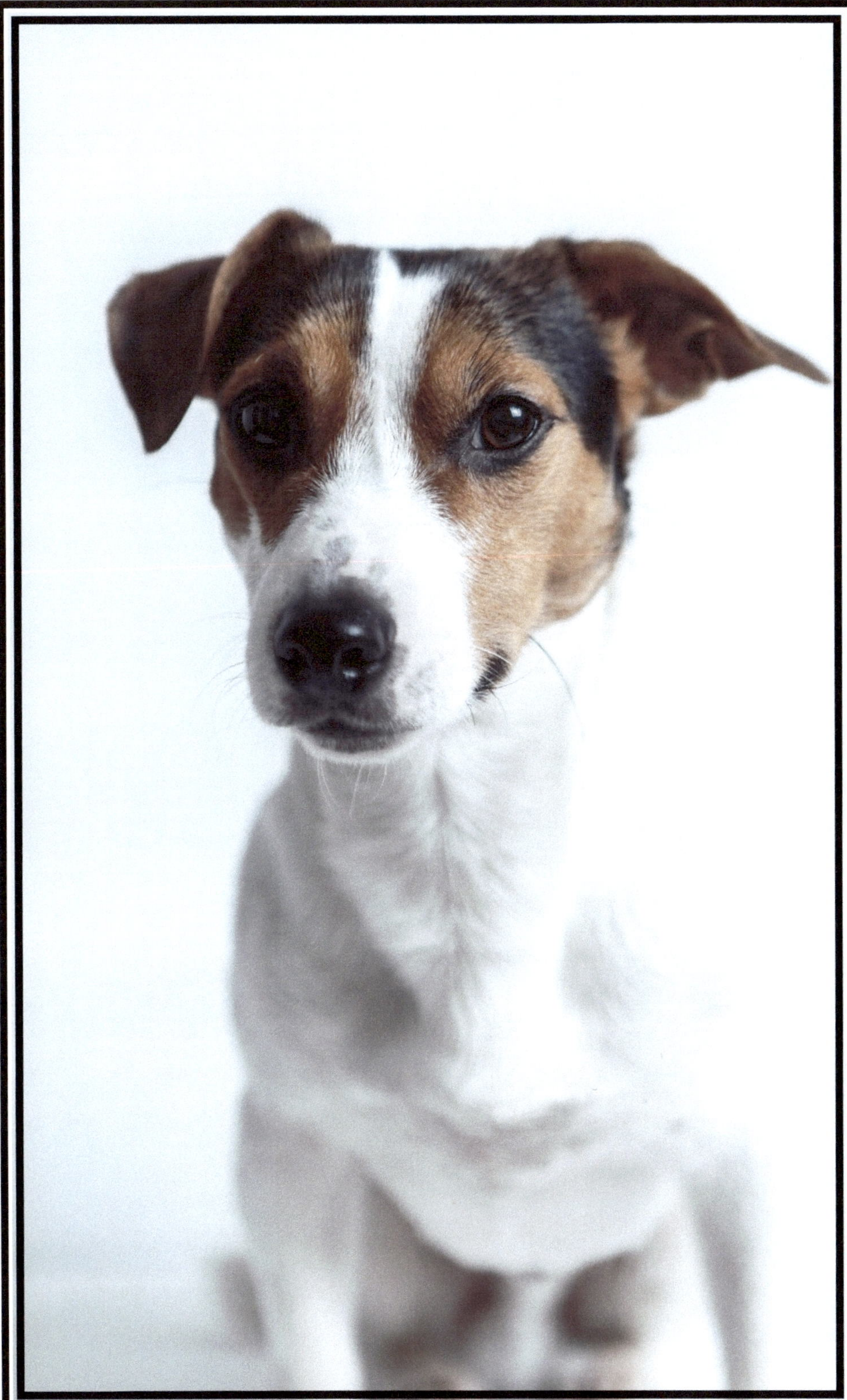

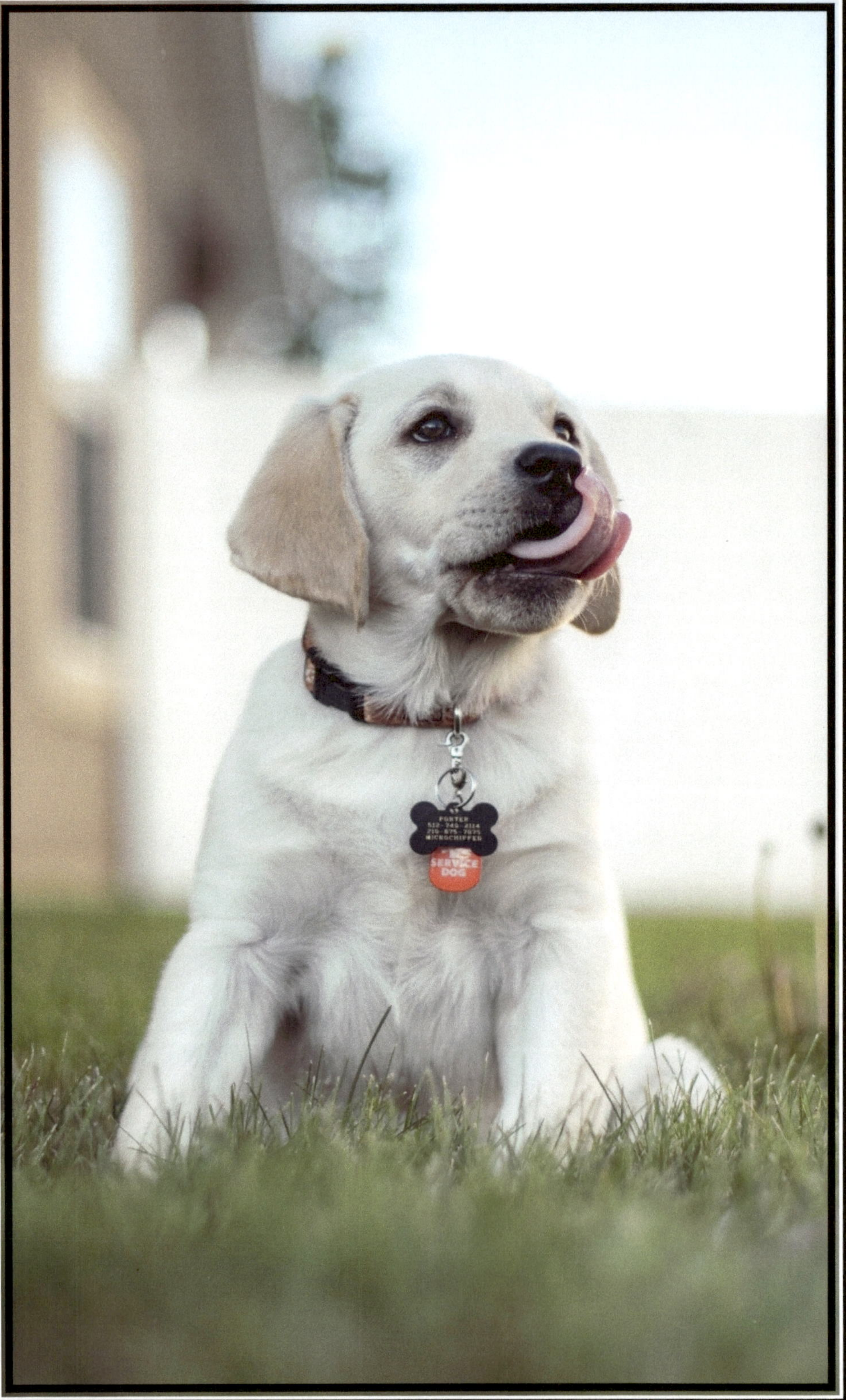

PORTER
512-749-2114
210-875-7075
MICROCHIPPED
SERVICE DOG

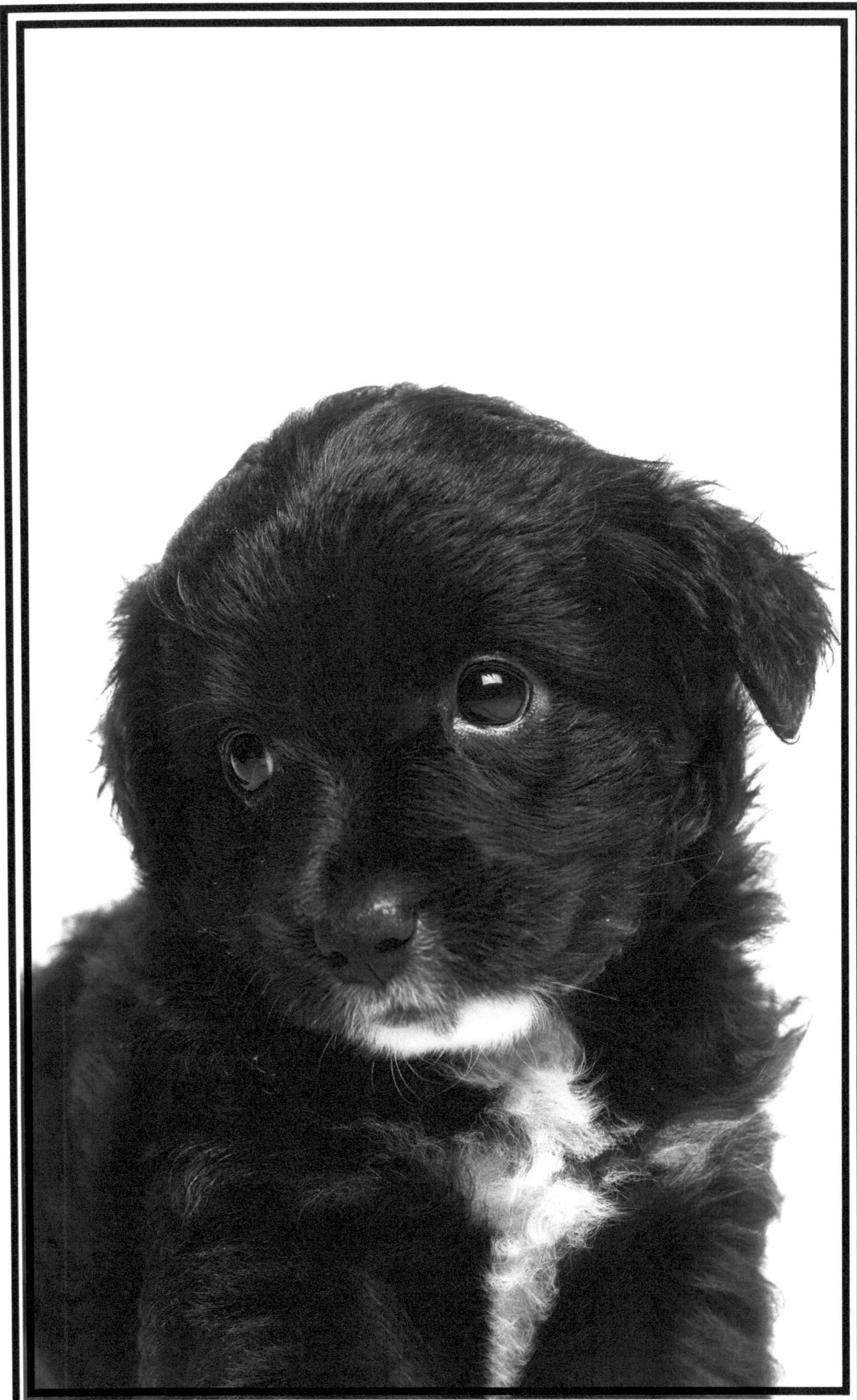